BEHAVIORAL ECONOMICS *for* LEADERS

MATTHIAS SUTTER

BEHAVIORAL ECONOMICS *for* LEADERS

RESEARCH-BASED INSIGHTS ON THE **WEIRD, IRRATIONAL,** AND *wonderful* **WAYS HUMANS NAVIGATE THE WORKPLACE**

WILEY

Copyright © Carl Hanser Verlag GmbH & Co. KG 2020, Munich 2022
Translated by: Marc Svetov

Published by John Wiley & Sons, Inc., Hoboken, New Jersey.
Published simultaneously in Canada.

For general information on our other products and services or for technical support, please contact our Customer Care Department within the United States at (800) 762-2974, outside the United States at (317) 572-3993 or fax (317) 572-4002.

Wiley also publishes its books in a variety of electronic formats. Some content that appears in print may not be available in electronic formats. For more information about Wiley products, visit our web site at www.wiley.com.

Library of Congress Cataloging-in-Publication Data

Names: Sutter, Matthias, author.
Title: Behavioral economics for leaders : research-based insights on the
  weird, irrational, and wonderful ways humans navigate the workplace /
  Matthias Sutter.
Description: First Edition. | Hoboken, NJ : Wiley, [2022] | Includes index.
Identifiers: LCCN 2022034799 (print) | LCCN 2022034800 (ebook) | ISBN
  9781119982975 (hardback) | ISBN 9781119982999 (adobe pdf) | ISBN
  9781119982982 (epub)
Subjects: LCSH: Economics—Psychological aspects. |
  Leadership—Psychological aspects. | Teams in the
  workplace—Psychological aspects.
Classification: LCC HB74.P8 S8813 2022 (print) | LCC HB74.P8 (ebook) |
  DDC 302.3/5—dc23/eng/20220721
LC record available at https://lccn.loc.gov/2022034799
LC ebook record available at https://lccn.loc.gov/2022034800

Cover Design: Wiley
Cover Image: © aleksandarvelasevic/Getty Images

SKY10038190_110822

*I dedicate this book to my wife Heidrun
and our daughters, Charlotte and Constanze.*

Contents

Acknowledgments

I want to thank Richard Narramore and Jessica Filippo from Wiley for their excellent guidance and many useful ideas on how to improve the book. Special thanks are due to Marc Svetov for his smooth translation and to Kim Wimpsett as a very thorough development editor. Without you, this book would not have been possible.

At some points in this book, I showcase my own research projects, which would not have seen the light of day without the marvelous collaboration of my co-authors on those projects. I would like to express my gratitude to Loukas Balafoutas, Andrej Gill, Daniela Glätzle-Rützler, Werner Güth, Stefan Haigner, Matthias Heinz, Jürgen Huber, Sabrina Jeworrek, Michael Kirchler, Martin Kocher, Maria Vittoria Levati, Vanessa Mertins, Wolfram Rosenberger, Heiner Schumacher, Matthias Stefan, Charlotte Sutter, Stefan Trautmann, and Eline van der Heijden.

Some of these research projects could be implemented only with the financial aid of research organizations, in particular, the Austrian Science Foundation ("Der Wissenschaftsfonds," FWF), the Anniversary Fund of Oesterreichische Nationalbank (OeNB), and the German Research Foundation ("Deutsche Forschungsgemeinschaft," DFG) as part of the Excellence Strategy—EXC2126/1-390939966 (ECONtribute Excellence Cluster).

The Max Planck Society deserves special thanks because it has been offering me excellent working conditions since 2017. At the Max Planck Institute for Research on Collective Goods in Bonn, I would like to thank the members of my "Experimental Economics Group," and especially Heidi Morgenstern and Zita Green for their outstanding collaboration. I'm grateful to the Universities of Cologne and Innsbruck for allowing me to continue to be part of these institutions, which I highly esteem, within the scope of short part-time contracts.

I thanked the three most important people in my life in the dedication.

Introduction: Why Do Smart People Behave Strangely?

Why do taller people get a higher salary? Why do women request a salary raise less frequently than men? Does enough money lure us to ignore all our moral concerns? Why do smart people behave strangely?

This book shares fascinating insights and findings of *behavioral economics*, a relatively new discipline in cutting-edge economic science. Behavioral economics uses empirical methods to comprehend the motives of human actions and uses a scientific framework for understanding strange and surprising aspects of professional life. This includes topics relevant to entry-level professionals, such as to what extent it is important to be the first or last to be interviewed for a job, as well as topics that are relevant to executives up to the board level, such as the question of why social skills play an ever more vital role in professional life as you rise in an organization. Controversial issues are also examined, such as whether hiring and promotion quotas are justified in companies and whether salaries ought to be public.

Behavioral economics is primarily based on economic experiments, where actual human beings make decisions under precisely defined conditions that have real consequences (e.g., in the form of money, prestige, or other intangible rewards). By systematically varying the conditions, you can get a good idea of what really drives human behavior and how people react in different conditions, regardless of how they explain their own behavior.

Many of the findings described in this book are based on field experiments conducted inside "live" businesses and organizations. Later in the book, for instance, I describe a field experiment in which we leased a call center and hired about 200 people to work there. Along with field experiments, lab experiments play a crucial role in behavioral economics. They typically involve students in computer labs who are paid depending on the decisions they make. Although field experiments are closer to the reality of everyday life, lab experiments are an indispensable supplement to the study of human behavior. One of the book's chapters deals with a study I conducted on the impact of gender quotas on women's willingness to compete.

Both field and lab experiments are always concerned with the question of how human behavior responds to incentives (monetary and nonmonetary) since this is what our professional life, from start to finish, is about. This book identifies curious and troubling human behaviors at all stages, from entry level to late career, with observations and insights that are relevant to both individuals and organizations.

For more than 20 years, the stages of professional life have been my focus of research in behavioral economics. What I found was often surprising, contradicting my expectations (e.g., the impact of quotas). This is why I love this field of research; I can challenge my own expectations—sometimes my prejudices—by looking at empirical data and revising them if needed.

When I applied for a position as a student assistant more than 25 years ago, the first step I took was to go to a bookstore to find specialist literature on "how to write a résumé" and "how to interview well." When, a few years ago, I was appointed director of a Max Planck Institute with nearly 100 employees, I looked into books on efficient staff management and guides on staff appraisals.

Although the guides somewhat helped me in both cases, I also realized that their point of view was limited, sometimes one-sided. What I was missing was something like an overriding and far-seeing idea about which factors are really important in professional life—for entry-level professionals and people about to retire; for middle-level managers and members of the board; for employees and employers alike; and for men and women to an equal extent in all these different roles. This greater insight is what I term the "human factor" in this book, the fact—trivial

only at first glance—that our working life always concerns falli-
ble, complicated human beings. You often need to take a closer
look at it to understand what it's about.

Over the last couple of decades, behavioral economists
worldwide have brought to light a cornucopia of answers to the
question of why smart people behave strangely. I share these
insights with you in this book and hope you will find them as
revealing and exciting as I do; they're sometimes surprising but
always thought-provoking!

Before we start, a brief instruction guide on how to use this
book: Each chapter presents a key finding that can be read and
understood independently of the other chapters. Many of the following 50 chapters start with a short story to illustrate the chapter's theme. The stories are mostly fictitious. (To distinguish fictitious characters from real people, only the real people have first
and last names; fictitious characters are identified only by their
first names.) I then explain what's interesting or important about
the story, in light of current research, and suggest applications
for everyday working life.

I wish all readers, from young professionals starting their career to experienced employees all the way up to the CEO, a great
and profitable reading experience.

Matthias Sutter

PART I

Behavioral Economics for Your Career

CHAPTER 1

The Taller You Are, The Higher Your Salary?

*S*alary depends on many factors, such as education, prior professional experience, and the assumption of management responsibilities. Your height should be irrelevant, but the crazy thing is, it seems to matter.

When you look at the executive and supervisory boards of major German public companies, what you see is primarily relatively tall men. Frank Appel of Deutsche Post is 6'6". At approximately 6'2", Michael Diekmann from Allianz is also above average. Most of the American presidents since World War II were taller than the average American male. Generals in the military usually are pretty tall as well. Even Napoleon, allegedly of small stature, is said to have been taller than his average soldier.

So it seems successful men are taller than average. It's known from labor market research that taller men also earn substantially more money on average than shorter men do. But while height may actually be an advantage on the battlefield, the question is: Why should taller men earn more anywhere else? The height of a manager, IT expert, or entrepreneur should be irrelevant to his salary. The data tells a different story. Studies from the United States and the United Kingdom show that men who are 4 inches taller than average earn about 10% more salary a year. Extrapolated to an entire working life, that difference in income easily adds up to six and seven digits!

Andrew Postlewaite from the University of Pennsylvania and his colleagues investigated why height has a positive impact on income. They examined two sample groups of men in the United States and the United Kingdom who were born in the late 1950s or early 1960s. Since the employment careers of women from these cohorts differ from those of men, the influence of height can be estimated more precisely for men, so Postlewaite and colleagues exclusively analyzed men. But height also plays a positive role for women. In the case of female twins, the taller twin earns several percentage points more than the shorter twin.

When trying to explain the influence of height on salary, we might begin with a naive assumption that employers prefer taller people and therefore pay them more. In earlier times, this might have been a reasonable argument in the military or in industry—before most physically demanding work was done by machines. In our highly industrialized economy, though, this is no longer so. There must be other reasons. A second guess would be that taller men come from different families than smaller men, which accounts for the pay differences. Indeed, shorter men are often from families with more children, where the parents had less education than the parents of taller men. But even if you take these family background differences in the statistical analysis into account (e.g., by looking only at men from families with the same number of children and the same level of education of their parents), it still turns out that 4 inches more in height makes for almost a 10% difference in salary. The review of other hypotheses confirms that this correlation is sustained even if you take into consideration health and cognitive abilities (such as intelligence tests).

Postlewaite's study made two fundamental findings in its further analysis. First, it's not the height in adulthood that matters but the height as a teenager, that is, at the age of 15 to 16. Some teenagers are already relatively tall by then; others go through a growth spurt later. Those who are relatively tall at that age earn more later than those who are shorter in their teens, regardless of their height in adulthood. A later employer normally possesses no information about the height of an employee as a teenager, so it can't be of any significance to the employer (and it has nothing to do with the intelligence quotient).

The second finding of Postlewaite gets to the heart of the matter. Taller teenagers have more social activities and contacts. They are, for instance, more often members of all sorts of clubs (sports or cultural ones, e.g.) or of student organizations. This fosters and trains so-called noncognitive abilities such as the capability of working on a team, endurance and stamina, ability to compromise, and leadership skills. Such qualities are of great importance in professional life. When you consider teenage activities in the analysis, there's no longer a statistically significant correlation between height and salary, Postlewaite's study proves. Height helps in the acquisition of social skills as a form of human capital, and this human capital leads to higher salaries in adulthood.

Takeaways

It's generally assumed that salary depends on people's skills and previous professional experience. But height also plays a role, at least for men. Taller people build up larger social networks in their late teens and acquire more social skills. This results in higher salaries later in life.

References

Persico, N.; Postlewaite, A.; Silverman, D.: (2004) The effect of adolescent experience on labor market outcomes: The case of height. Journal of Political Economy, 112: 1019–1051.

CHAPTER 2

The Job Interview—It's Tougher for Women

*E*quality between women and men in the labor market is far from perfect. It starts with the job interview, in which women are already at a disadvantage. Let's take a look behind the scenes of the arts, entertainment, and academic hierarchies.

The violinist steps on stage and walks toward the center. The floor is covered with a thick carpet. Nobody is on the stage but the violinist. The curtain to the auditorium is closed. Via a loudspeaker, she is asked to start playing. The woman has opted for a piece by Johann Sebastian Bach. Fully concentrating, she lowers the bow onto the strings and commences. The melody sounds heavenly. But who's listening?

Five people sit behind the curtain in the auditorium who pay close attention to every note. They have no idea who is currently auditioning for the open position of a violinist in their orchestra, whether a man or a woman is playing, whether the person is young or old, whether they are white or a person of color. Since the thick carpet on the stage floor absorbs the sound of steps, the jurors cannot guess the gender of the violinist by listening to the clacking of high heels. The five people simply have the task of finding the best qualified person—of any gender—for the vacancy.

Today, many orchestras around the world handle auditioning for a vacancy like this. To ensure equal opportunity for all genders, musicians of any, white people or people of color, the auditioning is *blind* as it's called. This means the selection panel makes its decision on who will get the job solely based on what it hears. Does this boost a woman's chances of being hired?

Data on the filling of vacancies in the top American orchestras—such as the Chicago Symphony Orchestra and the New York Philharmonic Orchestra—shows that blind auditioning has made a significant contribution to more women being hired. Compared to hiring procedures without blind auditioning, the anonymity of an audition increases the likelihood by around 50% that women will make it to the next round in a multistage selection process. When it comes to the last round, women end up prevailing almost twice as much in a blind audition than without anonymity. In other words, blind auditioning avoids discrimination due to gender.

Although many orchestras are turning to this approach, normally corporate hiring processes are not blind. Quite the contrary. Usually, when someone applies for a job, the name on a résumé or an in-person job interview inevitably betrays personal attributes such as gender, age, and race. Of course, when filling a vacancy, the personal impression a candidate makes is important in addition to professional qualifications. Most people think the "chemistry" must be right between all parties involved in the recruitment process. However, it can be empirically proven in this context that thinking the recruiter can ignore the gender of an applicant is an illusion. One reason for this is the gender makeup of hiring committees, as new studies on academic promotions in Italy and Spain suggest.

In both countries, candidates for vacant academic chairs must undergo selection procedures organized by the government; in other words, they have to present themselves to a panel of academics in their fields. Based on more than 100,000 application procedures with more than 8,000 panel members, Manuel Bagues of the University of Warwick and colleagues investigated how the chances for a woman being hired were impacted by how many women were sitting on the selection panel. As a gut reaction, you might think that a greater share of women on the panel would be an advantage for female candidates. Italy and Spain, nonetheless, don't corroborate this assumption. On the contrary, having more women on the panel actually reduces the chances of success for female candidates, albeit only to a slight extent.

The explanation is that although female panel members evaluate female candidates better on average than their male counterparts, female candidates are evaluated substantially more harshly by male panelists as soon as there are women on the panel. This result appears to indicate that men on selection panels have a tougher attitude toward hiring female candidates *because* other women are already sitting on the panel who have made it "to the top." Mandatory quotas for the number of women on important decision-making entities (e.g., selection panels) are obligatory in many fields, not only in academia. This might have unintended and undesirable consequences for female candidates looking for a position.

Takeaways

Women are evaluated more negatively by men in job interviews if the proportion of women in responsible positions is already relatively high. Therefore, more women on staff selection panels often pose a certain disadvantage for female applicants.

References

Bagues, M.; Sylos-Labini, M.; Zinovyeva, N.: (2017) Does the gender composition of scientific committees matter? American Economic Review, 107: 1207–1238.

Goldin, C.; Rouse, C.: (2000) Orchestrating impartiality: The impact of "blind" auditions on female musicians. American Economic Review, 90: 715–741.

CHAPTER 3

Working from Home Is Great— But It May Hurt Your Career

*T*he COVID-19 pandemic produced an unprecedented shift *in the location of work by forcing millions, perhaps billions, of people to work from home. While before the pandemic working from home was often viewed skeptically, now it is widely embraced. So, we are beginning to understand its pros and cons better, in particular, also what it means for your career.*

Brian has been working as a language editor at a prestigious research institution for several years. With the advent of the COVID-19 pandemic, he has shifted to working from home for the entire week, while before the pandemic he was usually in the office for four days. When the pandemic hit workplaces world-wide, Heidi, his boss, was not sure whether Brian would work equally well and productively from home as he always did in the office. Given that the young researchers benefit considerably from his revisions of their scientific texts, it is important for their publication, and thus career prospects, that Brian is doing his job as excellently as he did before the pandemic. So far, Heidi and the researchers, as well as Brian, have been very satisfied with the new work arrangements.

Even before the pandemic, the use of the home office was on the rise worldwide. In the United States, for instance, the proportion of employees who work remotely on some days of the week has risen fivefold over the past 30 to 40 years before the pandemic hit the world. Similarly, in Germany and Austria, around 50% of employees worked from home, albeit usually only one day a week. With the pandemic, the number of people working from home has further increased, reaching levels that would have seemed impossible—and to many unacceptable—before the pandemic. Of course, this development has not only been somewhat forced on us due to social distancing restrictions, but due to an increasingly digitized world, the place of work has also become increasingly irrelevant. The trend toward working from home is also welcome for environmental reasons, since it reduces commuter traffic between home and the workplace.

From an employee's perspective, working from home improves work-life balance. On the employers' side, they benefit from needing less office space and thus save money. Yet, many employers may be skeptical whether employees work sufficiently well from home. Employee interest groups see a risk of employees becoming isolated and lonely if they work too much from home. Depending on which perspective one takes, working from home is judged as rather positive or negative by employers or employees.

One of the problems of how to assess working at home is that there is hardly any evidence of causal effects because virtually all studies are flawed by a selection problem. This means that people who request to work from home and use the opportunity to do so are not the same people as those who don't. In an ideal situation, either you allow the people who want to work from home to do so or you force them to continue to work in the office at the company's premises. This would get rid of the selection problem, and the causal effect of working at home would be measurable as long as the activities to be done in the office or at home are practically identical.

Even before the pandemic's onset, a study conducted by Nicholas Bloom of Stanford University and a group of coauthors met these conditions. Around 1,000 employees at the Shanghai branch of the largest Chinese travel agency CTrip were able to choose if they wanted to work in their home offices four days a week. The group of 500 employees who were interested was randomly divided into two subgroups. Two hundred and fifty employees had to work from home four days a week for nine months, while the other half had to show up at the office all five days. The work was the same for both groups: taking telephone calls and booking individual trips, package tours, and business trips. Payment and working hours were identical for both groups; only the workplace differed.

During the nine months, work productivity rose 13% due to remote work, largely owing to the fact that fewer breaks were taken there and to a lesser extent because a higher number of telephone calls were handled per shift. Job satisfaction of the people working from home was also greater, and they stayed with the company far longer. So far, so good. However, the home office had a serious disadvantage that became apparent only when the data was analyzed in greater detail: Promotions (e.g., to team leader) were much more frequently given to employees working in the office at the company. Natalia Emanuel and Emma Harrington from Harvard University revealed a similar effect in a study—run during the pandemic—about a major on-line retailer in the United States. Productivity in the home office increased nearly 8% but the likelihood of being promoted when working at home declined by more than 10% points.

Fewer opportunities for advancement are therefore a side effect of the home office that ought not be underestimated. Networking to further one's career is just easier in the office than from home, so the study by Bloom and his coauthors showed that the vast majority of home-office employees wanted to return to the company office. From the company's point of view, the home office paid off nicely, owing to the rise in productivity.

Based on the experience gained during the pandemic, it can be expected that the home office will remain an essential part of our working lives. Work by Nicholas Bloom and coauthors or by Emanuel and Harrington shows us that is not only good or not only bad—the crucial point is that the pros and cons for employers and workers be well balanced.

Takeaways

Working from home increases productivity in many instances and boosts job satisfaction because it helps sustain the balance between family and work, while eliminating the hassle of the daily commute. However, working from home also entails the risk that promotions will become less likely since networking is a lot more difficult.

References

Bloom, N.; Liang, J.; Roberts, J.; Ying, Z. J.: (2015) Does working from home work? Evidence from a Chinese experiment. Quarterly Journal of Economics, 130: 165–218.

Emanuel, N.; Harrington, E.: (2021) "Working" remotely? Selection, treatment and the market provision of remote work. Working Paper. Harvard University.

CHAPTER 4

Social Skills Are Worth More Now Than 10 Years Ago—Much More

Training in terms of professional content alone no longer suffices for a permanent job and a good salary. In addition to technical or analytical skills, you had better bring along a few social skills to the job, for instance, to be able to coordinate your work with other team members or find compromises in difficult situations. Such skills are increasingly in demand on the labor market and definitely add something to salary rates.

At the onset of my career as an academic, I had the idea—with hindsight, a naive one—that successful research depends solely on good ideas and that these ideas would prevail almost automatically in the medium and long terms. I wasn't aware then that you have to present your ideas to your colleagues in the international academic community at regular intervals, that you have to defend them with verve, and that you have to adapt and improve them in response to feedback. The relevance of this social process for successfully publishing in the top journals of economics became clear to me only little by little. One other thing I had to learn about 25 years ago was that good research emerges increasingly from teamwork and that in few cases is it the work of an individual. I was lucky to find a brilliant partner in Martin Kocher, today the Austrian Minister of Labor and Economic Affairs. Together, we were able to improve our research projects by discussing ideas over a cup of green tea and identifying weak points critically and openly—sometimes one of us had to convince the other guy that a different path was more auspicious. We divided the individual work steps of a project between us, which boosted our productivity enormously. We were always aware that we would look for a compromise when our opinions differed—and this is why we always found one. The morning meetings over a cup of tea taught me early on how important social skills are in the world of work today.

Recent research from labor economics confirms the importance of social skills and demonstrates that they have become even more relevant over the last 30 years. This is because that the portion of routine activities has been declining, at least in advanced industrial countries. Fewer and fewer activities can be carried out according to a rigid plan. In tandem with this development, social skills have become increasingly important. Social skills are basically defined by four factors.

- The knowledge that you have to coordinate the activities of different people to carry out the work steps efficiently.
- The ability to find a balance or compromise in the event of conflicting interests.
- The ability to convince people of better solutions.
- The insight that other people often have a different perspective on issues and the willingness to put yourself in their shoes.

David Deming of Harvard University used data on the careers of more than 10,000 Americans to investigate how and to what extent social skills pay off on the job market. His data set included information on the education of the people concerned as well as questionnaire data on their social skills. His analysis revealed that education and training—more generally, cognitive skills—of the people studied played a vital role. Those with higher education are far more likely to have a (full-time) job and earn more money. These findings are not surprising and are practically valid worldwide. Yet, regardless of cognitive abilities, social skills have a measurable effect as well. If you keep the cognitive skills constant and compare somebody with average social skills to a person among the 20% with the best social skills (based on a social skills index), the latter is 5% more likely to have a (full-time) job and earns 4% more money. Also remarkable is the fact that social skills bring more for people with higher education than for people with lower education. Education and social skills thus complement each other. If you are more capable, higher positions will be open to you, and in these positions you must be able to deal with people to work productively.

Another important insight from Deming's work is the fact that social skills have translated increasingly into financial benefits over the last few decades. If you compare employees aged 25 to 35 in the late 1980s with those of the same age in the late 2000s, the wage boost for social skills (given that the levels of education and the industry are the same) has roughly doubled. In the 1980s, better social skills led to a salary increase of only about 2% 10 years ago, it was already 4% Social skills are therefore paying off more and more, and this trend will continue and intensify in the future.

Takeaways

> The more complex the world of work becomes, the more valuable social skills are because jobs increasingly require efficient coordination of team members, facilitating their different wants and ideas and resolving conflicts. Such skills are increasingly rewarded by the labor market and yield better career opportunities and higher salaries.

References

Deming, D.: (2017) The growing importance of social skills in the labor market. Quarterly Journal of Economics, 132: 1593–1640.

CHAPTER 5

Fifty Percent of People Find a New Job Through Their Social Networks—Weak Connections Matter More Than Strong Ones

*E*mbarking on a career is one of the most exciting times of your life. After many years of sitting in a classroom, the moment has come to put what you have learned into practice. Things don't go smoothly for everybody, though. After all, it's not so easy to find a job. Social networks can be a significant aid to a successful professional start.

Of course, a sound education constitutes the basis of any successful professional career. Income data collected by the Bureau of Labor Statistics in the United States clearly shows that people with a higher education usually have higher income and lower risk of unemployment. The average annual salary for high school graduates is about $37,000; for those with a bachelor's degree, it's $60,000; and for people with a doctorate, it's $90,000. So education pays off in our working lives. Of course, the figures mentioned here refer to people actively engaged in a professional life, who have overcome the obstacles of entry in the labor market. The figures don't reveal anything about how this entry can be achieved. Entry, however, is an important obstacle on the path to professional success.

In the United States, some 20% of interviewees say that they ask their families and relatives for advice and help when looking for work. More than 50% say they found their job through their social networks. This is confirmed by the fact that a majority of American firms have *referral programs* in place, in which people already working in the company are asked to make recommendations about who might be a suitable job candidate. Social networks play a fundamental role in placing employees or finding jobs. Two intriguing studies demonstrate how.

Together with her coauthors, Laura Gee at Tufts University has studied more than 6 million Facebook accounts to check whether this social network plays a role in where to find a job, whether it's important to have close or weak connections to other people in your own network, and whether it's better to have many or few of each. The strength of the connection can be measured by the frequency with which two people send messages to each other or by the number of contacts they share ("friends"). Gee was able to show that the sturdier the connection, the greater the likelihood of two people working at the same company. Strong, close connections thus have a powerful impact on finding a certain job at a certain company. Yet, what's intriguing is that, overall, most people find employment through relatively weak contacts (with little messaging and few common friends). What at first glance seems paradoxical—sturdier connections have a stronger impact in a single case, but weaker connections have a greater impact overall—can be explained by the fact that the vast majority of people have only a few very close, sturdy contacts and a great many relatively weak ones. Through these weak contacts, owing to the greater social distance, they get information they wouldn't have access to normally. This means that weaker contacts are also vital in finding a job.

A recent study by Laurel Wheeler of the University of Alberta and her coauthors provides evidence that, for the most part, social networks help less educated and poorer people find a job. Wheeler and her group did a controlled field study in which job seekers (in poor neighborhoods in South African cities) were randomly divided into two groups for a career entry program lasting six to eight weeks. During the six to eight weeks, one group was introduced for four hours to LinkedIn, the world's largest professional network; they learned, for instance, how to open an account, link to other people, post entries there, describe qualifications well, and have them confirmed by other people. The other group was not given such training (although half of the people in this group had an account with LinkedIn). The training for the first group entailed a 10% greater likelihood of getting a job after finishing the program. The difference between the two groups was still nearly the same a full year after the program wrapped up. The reasons for the success of the first group with LinkedIn training are probably multifarious. The people in this group were searching for jobs full time and on a broader basis; they studied the professional profiles of other people more thoroughly (competitors on the labor market); and they created more compelling profiles for themselves and had a larger network of contacts. Networks are helpful because a significant proportion of vacancies are filled by recommendations from other people already working in the company.

Takeaways

> Social networks help you get started because valuable information on the opportunities offered on the labor market are conveyed through them. Close contacts are especially helpful, but there are a lot fewer of them than weaker contacts. Training in how to handle social networks can significantly increase career opportunities.

References

Gee, L. K.; Jones, J.; Burke, M.: (2017) Social networks and labor markets: How strong ties relate to job finding on Facebook's social network. Journal of Labor Economics, 35: 485–518.

Wheeler, L.; Garlick, R.; Johnson, E.; Shaw, P.; Gargano, M.: (2022) LinkedIn (to) job opportunities: Experimental evidence from job readiness training. American Economic Journal: Applied Economics, 14: 101–125.

CHAPTER 6

When Finding a New Job, Rigidly Structuring Your Day Is a Power Move

*I*t's not easy to find new work. In some countries, behavioral economists advise public employment agencies to help unemployed people to find work again. How does it work?

David Cameron, the former British prime minister, will probably go down in history as the man who initiated the Brexit referendum. But one of his projects was an experiment in behavioral economics—the installation of a so-called nudging unit in his government. The unit consisted of a group of economists and psychologists known as the Behavioral Insights Team, which dealt with the question of how government policies can be implemented in a more efficient, resource-saving, and citizen-friendly way without having to amend laws. The idea was to use *nudging*—giving people a gentle push in the right direction so they change their behavior.

The most spectacular success achieved by the Nudging Unit was in tax administration. Simple public announcements, for instance, let everyone know that nine out of ten citizens pay their tax bills on time. This improved most people's feeling about paying their taxes, didn't cost much, and allowed the Treasury easily to collect tens of millions of pounds more. In addition to tax administration, the Nudging Unit was concerned with finding jobs for the unemployed.

In several districts, the Nudging Unit helped British employment services counsel job seekers differently. In contrast to traditional training courses and information on vacancies, advisers drew up a detailed daily routine to help the unemployed stick to a schedule. Here's an example:

7:30 a.m.: Get up.

8:00 a.m.: Eat breakfast and scour the job ads for vacancies.

9:00 a.m.: Study the five most intriguing ads more closely and find out details about the companies online.

10:30 a.m.: Write cover letters to the most attractive companies.

12:00 noon: Lunch.

2:00 p.m.: Revise résumé to attach to the cover letter.

3:30 p.m.: Compile application folder with all the necessary documents for the three most intriguing job offers.

The psychological concept behind this type of consultation is called *implementation intentions*. To be able to carry out your intentions—find work—you need to define the steps to get closer to the desired goal. The result is that unemployed people actually will invest time in looking for a job—something that surprisingly many unemployed people do far too little, although one might think they have lots of time. In the case of implementation intentions, a gentle push consists of guiding the individuals in question in the right direction by small and manageable steps and explaining to them the next step, whatever it may be. The program demonstrated that people who were advised in this way were more likely to find employment again than job seekers who were advised in the conventional way.

A labor market study from South Africa confirmed that drawing up plans helps in finding a new job. A plan has an impact on job seekers by inducing them to send out more applications and spread their applications across more industries than they would have done without specific plans for hunting for a job. The latter explains why these people get more invitations to job interviews, get more job offers, and have a higher likelihood (of nearly 30%) of being employed again five to twelve weeks after it's been suggested to them to draw up a plan.

Planning the day ahead for targeted and professional applications is one method to get invitations to interviews. Another option is to attend job fairs and take part in interviews there. Even though employment agencies around the world usually tell unemployed people about job fairs and provide them with interview appointments, such offers are often not followed up on. So how can you get people to seize the opportunity by going to a job fair that the agency recommends to them? A field study was conducted in England about this. By SMS message, job seekers were reminded of a job fair taking place near them. But not all recipients got the same message. In the standard message (variant 1), the recipient was informed of the location and time of the job fair as well as an appointment for an interview with a specific company. As an alternative to the standard message, a personalized version was sent in which either the recipient was addressed personally (variant 2) or the message had the signature of the employment agency agent (variant 3). Variants 2 and 3 raised the likelihood that the job seeker showed up for the interview, from around 10% to almost 20%. The fourth variant of the SMS message had the best effect, though. In this version, an agent pointed out explicitly that she made a real effort to arrange an interview appointment for the recipient, that she wishes the person lots of success in the interview, and that she requests a little feedback afterward. With this variant, the likelihood that the recipient would show up for the interview went up to nearly 30% three times the rate that the usual standard variant would have yielded.

Where did this improvement come from? The most successful variant appeals to the reciprocity of the recipient. In simple terms, *reciprocity* means "tit for tat." If the agent put much effort into arranging an appointment, this implies a moral obligation for the unemployed person to react to the agent's efforts and show up at the job interview.

Takeaways

The usual approach to job placement for an unemployed person starts with providing training for specific professional skills. Alternative approaches using behavioral economics are based on the knowledge that a structured day and reciprocity between the agent and the job seeker are crucial. Job seekers should take this into account when looking for a new job.

References

Abel, M.; Burger, R.; Carranza, E.; Piraino, P: (2019) Bridging the intention-behavior gap? The effect of plan-making prompts on job search and employment. American Economic Journal: Applied Economics, 11: 284–301.

CHAPTER 7

Better "Zappa" Than "Adams"—Why Coming Later Alphabetically Gives You an Unfair Advantage

*B*eing invited to a job interview is the first step to success. Little things can play a role—your last name, for instance.

I have been living with the last name of Sutter for more than 50 years. It is part of my identity, and I like it. Granted, as a kid at school I was not always so thrilled that my name begins with an *S*. Class lists are arranged alphabetically, so I was always quite near the end (usually third or fourth last). When the teacher distributed in-class tests, I always learned pretty late what my grade was. Compared with my fellow students who came before me in the alphabet, I had to cope with the uncomfortable suspense longer. Later I went through alphabetical waiting lines at the university and while serving in the military. This is why I thought my last name was more of a disadvantage than an advantage far into adulthood. This was reinforced by the fact that the names of authors are normally arranged alphabetically in my academic field. Sutter goes to the end of the list, while two of my esteemed co-authors, let's say Sule Alan and Gary Charness, are at its head.

Over the years, I saw my last name also has its advantages—namely, in job interviews. In most of the application procedures in which I took part—like positions as a professor at various universities—the order of the candidates was determined alphabetically by the appointment panel. In the absence of another clear-cut system, this is quite common in many procedures, even outside academia. The fact that it was my turn to be interviewed late in the procedure or last turned out to be positive for my chances. I couldn't complain about a lack of offers in my career. I pride myself that my success in application procedures had something to do with my academic achievements, but my last name has in all likelihood contributed a little bit to it. There is scientific evidence of this. Since I'm a great fan of classical music, I'd like to illustrate it using the example of a music competition, namely, the Queen Elizabeth Competition for piano held in Belgium, which is one of the most prestigious competitions. The list of previous winners includes such famous piano virtuosos as Vladimir Ashkenazy and Valery Afanassiev.

The competition consists of several stages. In the last, decisive stage, 12 pianists compete to win. The winner not only gets prize money but also promises for concert performances, a prestigious stepping stone for their career. The twelve participants of the final round perform on six different evenings; two a night showcase their proficiency. The panel of judges—similar to an academic appointment panel or a selection committee for vacancies in companies—is made up of experts in the field. Each panelist rates every finalist separately; the winner is then determined from the individual scores. The order in which the finalists perform is determined randomly such that one letter is drawn, and, starting with this letter, the list is sorted alphabetically. So if the letter drawn is M, initially all the finalists from M to Z perform and then those from A to L.

Anybody who made it into the finals of this music competition is among the best musicians of their age group. Since the order of appearance is random and it's pretty unlikely that the last name of the artist is somehow part of their skills, the performance sequence should actually have no influence on the result of the competition. But that's not so, according to research by Victor Ginsburgh and Jan van Ours. Of the two finalists who perform on the same day, the finalist who plays later is ranked higher on average by one position. So it's a clear advantage to perform later on a certain day or to take your turn later in job interviews. If the selection procedure spans several days—as in the case of the piano competition—then the first day is the worst for an appearance. In the piano competition, the two finalists of the first day are rated three positions lower on average than the finalists of the following days. I saw these results confirmed in my own research on the Ferruccio Busoni Competition in Bolzano, Italy. In the three-stage finals, the likelihood of making it into the next round was always greatest if you performed on the last day of the stage in question.

Although a random—often alphabetical—order of candidates for a vacancy or for winning a competition should play no role in the results, it is better to have your turn late. In academia, candidates for a hire are often interviewed in alphabetical order, in which case a last name later in the alphabet constitutes an advantage because experts or judges sitting on panels don't tend to give the best grades to the ones who appeared first. There might be somebody better coming afterward. The fewer people who come after you, the more examiners are willing to give top grades for very top-notch performances. The insights from academia are of more general relevance, however, because the sequence of interviewing for a job in companies matters irrespective of whether the order was determined alphabetically or according to some other criterion.

In addition to a good performance, success requires that notorious bit of luck. Sometimes the luck simply consists of having a last name that comes late in the alphabet or being invited to give one of the last interviews for an open position.

Takeaways

In application processes, the members of selection panels make comparisons among different candidates. The sequence of appearance plays a vital role because it's less likely that earlier candidates get good ratings than later candidates do when no one comes after them. That's why it's more favorable to be interviewed toward the end of the process.

References

Ginsburgh, V.; van Ours, J.: (2003) Expert opinion and compensation: Evidence from a musical competition. American Economic Review, 93: 289–296.

CHAPTER 8

Job Hunting and Patience

*L*ong interruptions in employment make it harder to return to the labor market. It's important to find employment quickly again after you've lost a job. Is patience helpful here or more of an obstacle?

Joining the line of the unemployed in front of an employment office looking for work is an unpleasant, sobering experience. At the beginning of my academic career, the austerity packages of the Austrian federal government in the 1990s resulted in all vacancies at universities being blocked. I had to make two trips to the employment office. Luckily, I was unemployed for only a short while. Labor market statistics show that people with higher education find a new job more quickly, so extended periods of time without a job are less frequent. Surprisingly, a higher salary before being unemployed also helps in finding a job. It shows that a person looking for work has been employed in a responsible, maybe even high, position, so the person in question has experience and expertise. And these qualities are attractive to the labor market.

Some personal qualities can also help in getting back to work. One is patience or the ability to work toward a goal and persevere no matter what the effort might be. For a long time, labor market researchers were uncertain whether patience was a virtue when looking for a job.

Some theorized that patient people would have an advantage, since patience helps with the stress and hassle, even if it doesn't entail immediate success. Impatient people tend to cease their efforts sooner since they tend to see unsuccessful job hunting not as an investment in the future but as a short-term, failed endeavor. Further, impatient people invest less time and energy in seeking employment, so they often get less attractive offers. This view would mean that patient people find a job more quickly.

Others argued that impatience can lead to relative success more quickly because impatient people are ready to accept lousier conditions, especially in terms of salary, to avoid having to go on a longer job search. In this hypothesis, they would find a new job more quickly than patient people who take the time to look for a better paid and more attractive job. According to this logic, impatient people accept lower-paid jobs but return to the labor market more quickly than more patient people.

Which of these views better reflects reality? Stefano della Vigna at the University of California, Berkeley, and Daniele Paserman of the Hebrew University of Jerusalem examined the correlation between the duration of unemployment and the patience of an unemployed person. They classified the impatience of employees based on information collected in questionnaires.

A first indicator of patience was whether somebody is a smoker. A smoker was more likely to be seen as impatient than a nonsmoker. There's ample evidence that smokers are more impatient when weighing the present and the future. In addition, della Vigna and Paserman collected data on the amount of money a person has saved. Having savings instead of debts was another indicator of patience. Although saving restricts immediate consumption, it allows for more consumption in the long run. So the existence of savings indicates a higher degree of patience. In addition to the information on smoking or the existence of savings, the authors of the study used a number of other indicators, for instance, whether a life insurance policy has been taken out or the assessment of the interviewer while questioning unemployed people. All these indicators are closely related and have been combined by della Vigna and Paserman into a measure for the level of patience an individual can muster. This measure was then correlated with the labor market data about the person in question.

The results of the study clearly show that more impatient people take longer to find a new job. One of the main reasons is they invest less in the job hunt so they don't even get lower-paid offers. Often they spend only a few hours a week hunting for a job—despite being unemployed. The small number of hours dedicated to job hunting might be explained by the fact that more impatient people are more easily discouraged because they find it harder to swallow negative feedback to an application and to face the risk of more rejection notices. It could also be they just find it hard to pick themselves up again and look for a job. Thus a vicious circle starts. People with less patience persevere for shorter periods in a profession and at a particular job and find a new job less quickly when they're unemployed. This may result in long-term unemployment and dropping out of the labor market. It's important to remain patient when looking for a job and have stamina in submitting your résumé. Discussing your situation with an expert at an employment agency can help enormously here, as shown in Chapter 6.

Takeaways

When looking for a new job, you have to invest a great deal of time and be able to withstand rejection. Impatient people have a harder time coping. This is why they take longer to find a new job than more patient, future-looking people.

References

Della Vigna, S.; Paserman, M.: (2005) Job search and impatience. Journal of Labor Economics, 23: 527–588.

PART II

Behavioral Economics for Hiring and Retaining Talent

CHAPTER 9

Startups with a Larger Share of Women Last Longer

*T*he staff of contemporary organizations is often diverse. *Younger and older employees, old-timers and new hires, people speaking different languages, people of different ethnic groups and genders. So what does the ratio of men and women in startup companies tell us?*

As a young man, my father worked at a small company in the Western part of Austria. All his colleagues came from the immediate geographical area, spoke the same dialect, and were mostly males because the employment rate of women was still far lower than that of men back in those days. In the years after World War II, the word *diversity* was still totally unknown. Nobody would have understood the idea, widespread today, that it might be profitable for companies to have employees with diverse backgrounds when it comes to language, ethnicity, and gender. Since employees were far less mobile at that time, a high degree of diversity wasn't even conceivable and therefore couldn't have been seriously taken in consideration.

Today it's a lot different. In academia—where I've been working for more than 20 years—it has become natural that research teams are made up of individuals from diverse groups of people. My inaugural working group at the Max Planck Institute in Bonn in 2018 included three Italian women, two Austrian males, one Bulgarian female, one German male, one South African woman, an American male, one Norwegian man, one Croatian man, and one Indian woman. I strove for a balanced gender ratio during the hiring process, yet I hadn't reflected much upon the question of whether diversity, in this case in terms of gender, would pay off. It seemed pretty difficult to measure for me as the head of a research group.

Diversity is widely encouraged, but what is the evidence that diversity is actually valuable to a company? Couldn't it lead to conflicts owing to different backgrounds? Although diversity means far more than just the single dimension of gender, a study on gender conducted by Andrea Weber and Christine Zulehner at the Vienna University of Economics yields valuable insights. The study analyzed the impact the share of women has on the longevity of startup companies. Weber and Zulehner did research on nearly 30,000 Austrian companies that were founded between 1978 and 2006, about which they had accurate data regarding the gender balance of their workforces. These companies covered a wide range of industries, for example, mechanical engineering and catering. Weber and Zulehner measured the share of women within the workforce as a whole at the point of the company's founding and the development of that particular share over the following quarters and years—until the company shut down, if it no longer existed at the time of the survey.

On average, every second company went bankrupt or discontinued operations after about six years. More important, the survival of a company vitally depended on how many women worked there. To illustrate this, Weber and Zulehner first standardized the share of women in a company using the industry average. The differences among industries can be considerable, so using the industry average as the standard, researchers determined whether relatively more or relatively fewer women worked in each company. Then Weber and Zulehner compared those companies that were among the 25% of companies with the least amount of women with firms that were close to the industry average. The results showed that the companies with the fewest women went bankrupt about 1.5 years earlier than companies with an average number of female employees according to the standard in the industry. Of the companies with the fewest women in the beginning, those that systematically boosted the share of women over the course of their existence, approximating it to the industry average, survived for a longer period of years. The gender-specific composition and corresponding development of the workforce have a consistent impact on the survival and success of a newly founded company.

How can these results be explained? A share of women far below the industry average pointed to gender discrimination, since it is to be assumed that talent for a particular profession is basically distributed equally between men and women. This doesn't mean that the interest men and women have for a particular sector has to be exactly the same. But within an industry, you'd expect that men and women would be equally suited. In the case of the companies with the lowest shares of women on their workforce, it can therefore be assumed that distortions play a role in the hiring process. Such distortions mean that the qualification and suitability of an applicant carry less weight in a recruitment decision. Extremes in the splitting of positions between the genders, for example, a definitely below-average share of women, indicate a suboptimal selection of staff. Apparently companies that don't want to adapt pay a price for their obstinacy: they go out of business sooner. Personnel decisions regarding diversity are therefore significant for the competitiveness of companies.

Takeaways

Many newly founded companies disappear from the market after a few years. Survival depends on the composition of the workforce. Startups survive for shorter periods of time if the share of women there is significantly below the average in their industry. A below-average share of women is likely to be a signal for distortions and bias in personnel selection.

References

Weber, A.; Zulehner, C.: (2010) Female hires and success of startups. American Economic Review, Papers and Proceedings, 100: 358–361.

CHAPTER 10

The Unintended Positive Side Effects of Employee Referral Programs

A *lthough employee referral programs are often criticized as nepotism, there are economic benefits for companies if vacancies are filled by people who were recommended by employees already working there. Some companies even pay the referrer a bonus. What is this all about?*

When supermarket cashier Mary enters the employee locker room one morning, she sees that a new sign has been put up on the bulletin board. In large letters, it states that employees will receive a bonus of $100 if vacancies are filled through their recommendations. In small print, it says that the bonus will be paid if both the referring person and the new hire remain in the company for at least five months. After reading the bulletin, Mary goes to the supermarket checkout line and starts her daily work. The first customers come in while Mary logs in at the register, unwraps the rolls of coins, and checks the paper money again. She has a long day ahead of her; but tonight, she thinks, she'll call her friend Sally, who is currently unemployed, and tell her about the vacancy at the supermarket. If Sally is interested, Mary will make a recommendation for Sally to the branch manager tomorrow. If all turns out right, both women can be helped: Sally with a new job and Mary with a bonus and a nice new colleague. Mary does not spend much time wondering why the supermarket chain is suddenly willing to pay a bonus for referrals. The retail chain likely has its own reasons.

It is indeed a huge challenge for companies to fill vacancies. The process of hiring a new employee takes a long time and is costly. Advertising for the job, going through the applications, conducting job interviews, drawing up the contract, training a new colleague, and integrating that person into the staff are only a few steps in the hiring procedure. All these things take time away from the existing staff and create costs for the company. For this reason, companies try to keep costs down and the accuracy of fit for new employees as great as possible when hiring.

Some companies avail themselves of computer algorithms to help with personnel selection (as described in Chapter 11). Another approach to personnel recruitment is soliciting recommendations from existing employees on who would be eligible for open positions. According to surveys, 70% of all American companies have so-called employee referral programs in place.

The potential benefits of such programs are multifaceted. Current employees might know quite well what the position requires and can assess who would be the right match to fill it. In addition, it can be anticipated that current employees will recommend only those with whom they get along well—another important factor for the working atmosphere in a company.

Empirical studies show that people who find a job through a referral from a current employee are hired more quickly, tend to be better qualified, and will stay longer with the firm than people who were not referred. The evidence is based on surveys among truck drivers, call center employees, and high-tech companies, for instance. In all these industries, however, the proportion of employees hired owing to recommendations from existing staff is relatively small, so it remains unclear initially whether referrals have a specific positive impact on companies. After all, recommendations also cost money when companies have a policy of paying bonuses if the new hire and existing employee stay with the company for a specified period of time, usually a few months.

Mitch Hoffman from Toronto University and colleagues in Cologne, Frankfurt, and Konstanz scrutinized company referral programs quite extensively. They analyzed a supermarket chain in the Baltic region, where every year almost 80% of employees quit their jobs. This means that the chain had to hire new people continuously, which was time-consuming and expensive. The company then launched a referral program at its 238 branches, employing more than 5,000 people. If the referral by an employee led to a new hire and the new person remained in the company for at least five months, the referrer was given €50, €90, or €120, depending on the location.

Although a higher bonus resulted in more recommendations, the proportion of new employees who joined the company on the basis of referrals remained less than 5%. So recommendations accounted for only a small portion of new employees.

Nonetheless, the program had a big impact, albeit an unexpected one. As shown in the aforementioned studies, the people recommended stayed with the company longer and had fewer sick days, but the main impact of the referral program was a different one. The current employees who made recommendations stayed longer with the company after the program was launched and were 15% less likely to terminate their jobs (compared to a control group of branches, where no referral program was initiated). These employees had a stronger feeling that they were taken seriously due to the launch of the program and appreciated that they had a say in hiring new personnel. Not only did employees stay longer at the company, but job satisfaction increased.

These previously overlooked side effects of referral programs pay off for a company—it's a win-win situation for employers and employees.

Takeaways

Filling vacancies is costly. Many companies request that their existing employees give recommendations on who is a good match for a position and a suitable addition to the team. The involvement of existing employees by means of referral programs increases their job satisfaction and the length of time they stay with the company.

References

Friebel, G.; Heinz, M.; Hoffman, M.; Zubanov, N.: (2022) What do employee referral programs do? Journal of Political Economy, in press.

CHAPTER 11

Managers Make Systematic Hiring Mistakes— Machines Can Help

*H*uman decision-making behavior is subject to systematic errors. This applies to the recruitment and hiring of new employees as other chapters in this book show. But can machine algorithms reduce hiring manager errors? Or is it better for a company if the heads of the HR department have sole discretion?

Mitch Hoffman of the University of Toronto studied these questions using data from 445 HR managers who had hired staff for a total of 90,000 positions in 15 North American companies. These companies supported their HR manager's hiring decisions with a sorting test and algorithm developed by a personnel consulting company that divided up applications into high potential (green), medium potential (yellow), and low potential (red). As part of the test, applicants were asked in a detailed questionnaire about their technical skills, their computer knowledge, their personality, and their cognitive abilities; in addition, they had to evaluate various professional scenarios. From this, the personnel consultants put applicants into the green, yellow, and red categories. The evaluation algorithm was based on tests from the past and the performance of previous candidates in their later jobs, in relation to productivity and how long they stayed with the company. The HR consultants specialized in jobs in the lower-skilled segment of the labor market such as data entry, working at a call center, or simple data analysis. Over the last few years, an average of 48% of all applications were classed as green, 32% yellow, and 20% red. The HR managers in the 15 companies were encouraged to pay heed to the color-coded application but had free power of discretion over whom they would ultimately hire.

Mitch Hoffman and his colleagues now wanted to find out whether the fact that a manager hired a "yellow" applicant even though a "green" one was available has a positive or negative impact later. Basically, the effect can go both ways. Greater power of discretion for managers makes it possible that they, based on their own experience, are better equipped than a computer algorithm to assess whether someone will fit into the company and the work team in question. At the same time, more power of discretion may result in the manager making decisions according to their personal biases rather than according to statistically calculated probabilities about which applicant is more promising.

The results of Hoffman and his team are sobering in terms of the human ability to make decisions in recruitment procedures. When HR managers used their years of expertise and discretion to go against the test results and the algorithm's recommendation and instead hire a lower-ranked recruit over a candidate with a higher test/algorithm score, those newly hired people stayed with the company for less time than when the HR manager followed the color recommendation. Colleagues hired despite the color recommendation also were not more productive—which would be a legitimate reason for deviating from the recommendation of the algorithm. Instead, they tended to be less productive.

The clear conclusion then is that giving HR managers too much power of discretion to override test and algorithm results may be a detriment for a company in terms of the quality of new employees and the period of time they stay with the firm, at least for this test and this segment of the labor market. Good hiring decisions can be supported by machines. This even applies if HR managers don't always follow the recommendations from the data. In companies that didn't receive machine hiring recommendations, the average stay of new employees fell, compared to those companies in which HR managers received color recommendations but were not forced to follow them. The existence of machine recommendations as such seems to push the recruitment decision in a positive direction.

Takeaways

Human decision-making behavior is subject to errors and distortions. Computer algorithms can help identify the best candidates from among a flood of applications. Taking machine recommendations into consideration may result in an improved selection of personnel and on how long employees stay with the firm.

References

Hoffman, M.; Kahn, L.; Li, D.: (2018) Discretion in hiring. Quarterly Journal of Economics, 133: 765–800.

CHAPTER 12

Why Employers Prefer Employees Who Don't Job Hop

*T*he average period of time employees stay at the same company is getting ever shorter. People are changing jobs more and more frequently. At the same time, employers value loyalty when they assess the résumés of potential job candidates. How does this affect people looking for work?

Mobility on the labor market is often perceived as a good thing. People who know how to exploit the opportunities of the labor market and collect experience in many companies are considered to be dynamic. Loyalty to a company, maybe even over decades, by contrast, seems to be an old-fashioned attitude that no longer meets the requirements of today's labor market. It is without a doubt true that it enriches your experience if you become familiar with different work routines, different organizational forms, different bosses and colleagues, or simply a different activity in another company.

But from the company's perspective, high employee churn entails high costs. New employees must be trained, they must be integrated into existing structures—without too many conflicts, if possible—and they must internalize the routines to make a contribution to the success of the department. It's time-consuming and costly. So when it comes to hiring somebody, it's vital to a company that the person can integrate in the new work environment and adopt the company's values. Along with the formal training of a job applicant, soft factors such as reliability, trustworthiness, ability to work on a team, loyalty, and perseverance play preeminent roles. These soft factors are hard to measure and review when hiring a new employee.

A study from Switzerland shows which data from a résumé is crucial to an HR manager when assessing these soft factors. It is the frequency with which otherwise perfectly comparable applicants have changed employers in their previous working lives. Changing your employee too often leaves a bad impression and reduces the chances of being invited to an interview in the first place.

Under the aegis of Roberto Weber from the University of Zurich, the Swiss researchers conducted a field study, in which, in response to more than 800 vacancies advertised in German-speaking Switzerland, two applications were submitted for each job. They created fictitious applicants, who were all 26 years old, had eight years of professional experience after completing a commercial college education with very good grades, spoke several (always the same) foreign languages, had similar names, and no unusual appearance. The researchers submitted two applications for each vacancy, which differed solely in the number of employers in the previous working life of the candidates. In one case, the applicant worked for the same company for the entire eight years after graduation; in the second case, the person changed employers every two years on average, so four employers were listed on his résumé. The four employers and the activities performed at the four firms were exactly comparable to the case of the applicant with only one employer.

In a first step, Weber and his team examined the question of how often the two different applicants were invited to an interview. At this point, there were already big differences. The applicant with only one employer was invited around 40% more often than the applicant with four employers on his résumé. In a second step, the authors of the study attempted to find out what caused these different rates of success in the applications. To do so, they interviewed 83 HR managers in Swiss companies, presented them with two different résumés listing either one or four employers, and had the managers assess the respective applicants. As you might expect, the applicants came off equally well in the categories of "skills" and "education"—after all, the résumés were deliberately designed to make the two candidates completely comparable in this respect. The assessment of the factors of "ability to work on a team," "perseverance," and "reliability" differed widely. Applicants with only one employer during the eight years after starting a career were consistently better judged in terms of these factors. They were deemed more likely to collaborate efficiently on a team; to work toward their goals with greater patience and persistence, even if they are hard to attain; and to be reliable in the fulfillment of their tasks.

These qualities are obviously important to potential employers. But since they cannot be measured directly and become apparent only in day-to-day work, employers interpret the number of job changes as an indication of how well an applicant does in terms of the soft factors.

The ability to stay with a company for longer may seem old-fashioned to some, but it might give you an edge in competing for a new job that may make all the difference between a job offer and a rejection.

Takeaways

Company loyalty signifies loyalty per se. Frequent job changes are often associated by HR managers with less loyal behavior and less dependability. This is why, if somebody seeks to change jobs, chances of a new position are reduced if that person worked for many different companies in the past.

References

Cohn, A.; Marechal, M.; Schneider, F.; Weber, R. A.: (2021) Frequent job changes can signal poor work attitude and reduce employability. Journal of the European Economic Association, 19: 475–508.

CHAPTER 13

Look for Candidates Who Demonstrate Patience and Long-Term Thinking

*E*mployee turnover has increased in recent years, and it's a real problem for employers. How can you tell whether somebody is going to stick around in a stressful environment? You'll find an answer in the world of truckers.

Driving a truck is attractive to some people because you get to travel to all corners of the continent. A few years ago, when I moved from the European University Institute in Florence to the University of Cologne and had my furniture delivered by a forwarding company, the truck driver told me enthusiastically that his job has already taken him from South Portugal to northern Norway and how he loved to be able to drive to the most remote corners of Europe. However, driving a truck is quite strenuous, characterized by fierce competition, tight schedules, short rest times, and not very family-friendly weekends at interstate rest stops, including snoozing in the sleeper cab. The driver of the trucking company told me that he had been suffering from persistent spinal disc problems. Still, he'd been doing it for more than 30 years, he said. What sets him apart from colleagues who quit a tough job much quicker?

Steven Burks from the University of Minnesota, together with several colleagues, approached the investigation of this question systematically. The authors conducted a study with 1,066 truckers as test subjects. They were trainees of a large American freight company. These trainees were trained in their job by experienced drivers and by instructional courses; during this time, they had to take on jobs for the company. The company paid all the training costs, which added up to $5,000 to 10,000 per trainee. If a trainee left the company before the end of 12 months, the training contract stipulated that the trainee had to repay all training costs.

Burks and his team conducted economic decision-making experiments with the 1,066 trainees during two training weeks. In these experiments, the trainees could always choose between two options. One option stipulated they would receive from $45 to $75 immediately. The other option was for them to get $80 but only later, the next day, for instance, or in four days or in four weeks. Based on their decisions about a smaller but immediate gain versus a larger but later gain, the trainees were classed into categories of being more or less patient (in terms of financial decisions).

The freight company provided the personnel data for every trucker involved to Burks and his team so they could link the experimental decisions—as a measure for patience—with the respective personnel data. The incentive for the company to take part in the study was to learn more about which factors have an impact on how long a trainee will stay with the firm—during and after the training period. The company profits from employees staying on for longer because only then can the initial training costs be made up for. From the personnel data, the authors of the study learned whether a driver had completed the training and, if not, how long they lasted. After completing the training, drivers were informed whether they would be hired by the company. While drivers who had completed their training were usually hired, drivers with disciplinary problems were not. For drivers who were given an employment contract, the authors of the study also learned how long the driver stayed with the company or whether he was still working there when the study was completed.

Trainees who were classified as more patient in the experiment because they opted for the larger but later sum were more likely to finish their training and more likely to be hired afterward.

In addition, drivers who made more forward-looking decisions (who more often chose the $80 option) stayed longer with the company after being given a job.

All in all, less than half of the drivers stayed on the job a full year or longer, even though a year was the minimum if you didn't want to pay your training costs. The drivers who reached the deadline were, on average, much more patient in their experiment decisions than those who ended the contract early and had to reimburse the company for the full training costs. For truck drivers who made more patient experimental decisions, staying on longer made sense financially since they didn't have to pay back training costs. The more impatient truckers not only had to repay the costs; the cards were also stacked against them in their professional life later. This is because impatience is a disadvantage when wanting to find a new job, as shown in Chapter 8.

Takeaways

> Day-to-day work can be stressful, and new challenges frequently crop up. Certain personal qualities help you not to give in too quickly when confronted with a challenge, but to tackle it and persevere. Patience and long-term thinking are two such valuable qualities.

References

Burks, S.; Carpenter, J.; Goette, L.; Rustichini, A.: (2009) Cognitive skills affect economic preferences, strategic behavior, and job attachment. Proceedings of the National Academy of Sciences, 106: 7745–7750.

CHAPTER 14

Unintended Negative Consequences of Salary Transparency

While in Scandinavia practically every citizen can view *the tax returns of their neighbor and thus their income, in most countries of the world income is one of the most closely guarded secrets. Public discussion on whether salaries ought to be disclosed flare up at regular intervals. What's not discussed in this context are the wanted and unwanted side effects that such pay transparency might have.*

A few years ago, the so-called Pay Transparency Act came into force in Germany with lots of concomitant media attention. The law requires companies with a certain number of employees on board to disclose upon request the criteria for salary classifications and provide information on how high the average salaries are in a particular position. When the law was adopted, it was hoped the law would help close the pay gap between men and women. At present it is still too early for a final assessment as to whether the law has helped in any way to achieve this goal. That data is not available yet. It's worthwhile, though, to take a closer look at the effects and side effects of more salary transparency in order to augment the political discussion—which is often partisan and can be dogmatic—by adding facts.

Analyzing the effects and side effects of salary transparency isn't an easy task. It requires that a situation with salary transparency can be compared to a situation without such transparency and that the two situations will differ as little as possible in all other aspects. A change in the law in California in 2010 made such a comparison possible. In California, it was decided that the individual salaries of public servants must be disclosed. The amendment was initiated after the media in California had reported some cases of exorbitantly high salaries for top officials in some cities and counties.

The 2010 amendment is quite suitable to study the impact of salary transparency because even before 2010, many cities and counties had published the salaries of their public employees. This means the salary development in the public sector can be analyzed from 2010 onward, depending on whether a municipality had published salaries already before 2010 or not. The different development in these two categories of municipalities allow a quantification of the impact of salary transparency.

Alexandre Mas of Princeton University took a closer look at this impact. In particular, he explored how the salaries of the top city officials evolved. In 172 cities, the salaries of top officials were published starting in 2010; in 296 cities, they had already done it prior to 2010. Alexandre Mas compared the salary development in these two groups of cities from 2009 (before the law took effect) up to 2012 (after the transparency law had been introduced). The first-ever publication of salaries in the 172 cities that made the salaries public only after 2010 resulted in a 7% reduction in salaries of the top city employees (compared to the development of salaries in cities that already published them prior to 2010). Since the salaries at the lower end of the scale were not affected by the obligation to publish, the law thus resulted in a compression of the salary pyramid. In other words, the differences between the highest and lowest salaries became smaller. From a European perspective—big salary differences are still less accepted in Europe than in the United States—this result might be deemed as both desired and desirable. Such a view, however, overlooks that the Californian law had two unwanted side effects.

For one, top officials quit their jobs twice as often after the publication of the salaries than in cities that had already been publishing salaries prior to that. At first glance, you might think the law had put a damper on excessive salaries, so top officials quit for that reason. But Alexandre Mas didn't find any statistical evidence that these officials had been overpaid compared with those in cities where salaries had already been disclosed before 2010. This suggests it was primarily media pressure that led to salary reductions, with the consequence that more top officials left office voluntarily.

Second, it took the cities concerned far longer to fill the vacancies of top officials than before. Instead of three months, filling positions after 2010 took an average of nearly five months. In addition, the new hires were significantly less qualified than their predecessors, resulting in financial losses for these cities in the long term.

This example underscores that the discussion about salary transparency must consider more aspects than just the disclosure of salaries. Like any medicine, salary transparency can have unwanted side effects. A relative salary scheme can have other types of side effects, as we will show in Chapter 37.

Takeaways

> The amount of one's own salary is one of the best kept secrets. For many, this is one of the reasons for gender differences in terms of pay, which is why some employees demand more salary transparency. If salary transparency is introduced for top positions in administration, it actually leads to more salary compression but makes it more difficult to fill senior positions.

References

Mas, A.: (2017) Does transparency lead to pay compression? Journal of Political Economy, 125: 1683–1721.

PART III

Behavioral Economics for Managers: Teamwork, Motivation, and Productivity

CHAPTER 15

Prejudiced Managers Hurt Employee Productivity— More by Neglect and Lack of Engagement Than Active Discrimination

*D*iscrimination *at the workplace can take many forms. It can target groups such as women or ethnic groups or older employees. Even if it is more subtle and not yet a criminal offense, discrimination can have a strong negative impact on the productivity of employees. The reason for this is surprising.*

Social psychologists have developed a test to measure stereotypes, prejudices, or the tendency to discriminate. The so-called implicit association test is based on the fact that the human brain associates two particular words more often with one another than others. For example, the terms *woman* and *family* are more quickly associated with each other than the terms *man* and *family*. The method for collecting the data for such associations is to have people confirm particular combinations of terms on a computer by pressing certain keys. The quicker the correct key is pressed, the stronger the associative links are between the two terms. *Woman* and *family* are far more quickly linked than *woman* and *career*, which says a great deal about the idea of women in our society.

The implicit association test can also be used to check whether stereotypes about certain groups prevail in working life and on the labor market. In a study involving Amanda Pallais of Harvard University, managers in a major French supermarket chain were tested with the implicit association test for how they assess the work performance of immigrants working at the supermarkets. Some 120 managers of the chain were asked to associate French or North African first names with positive or negative traits in employees. If positive traits were consistently associated more quickly with French first names, the implicit association test would indicate that the managers have certain expectations for the performance of employees of certain backgrounds. Indeed, the managers associated a good work performance far more quickly with French names. Whether these facts ought to be attributed to prejudice, stereotyping, or even discrimination against North African workers is initially a matter of the concepts used. From an economic point of view, the question is far more exciting of whether managers associate a good work performance with French or North African names more quickly or less quickly and what impact that has on the work performance of their subordinates. Then the attitudes of managers would have an impact on the productivity of the employees and thus on the profitability of the company.

To measure this, Pallais and her colleagues investigated the work performance of more than 200 cashiers in a French supermarket chain. About one-quarter of the (mostly female) cashiers had North African names, thus belonging to a minority. All cashiers were given a six-month contract. During the first six months, their working hours were assigned without their having a say in it. During a working day, it was largely coincidental which checkout manager a cashier had as supervisor. Managers who associated North African names more with a poor work performance in the test had a significant impact on the minority group's productivity. Cashiers with North African names were 50% more likely not to show up at work than those with French names if they had to deal with a more prejudiced manager. The same cashiers scanned about 2% fewer items a minute and needed 4% more time to scan the next customer's merchandise. In an initial reaction, this data might be interpreted as an indication of the lower productivity on the part of these cashiers. However, the cashiers from the minority group were actually more productive (i.e., faster and less frequently absent) than their colleagues with French names if they worked under a manager who showed no prejudice or only minor prejudices in the implicit association test.

So the attitudes of the managers had an impact on work productivity. But why? Following your initial impulse, you might think that managers with stronger prejudices treat members of the minority group in a less friendly way, demanded more overtime from them, or assigned more cleaning duties. Interviews with the cashiers, however, revealed no difference in this respect between those with French and those with North African names. Both groups felt they were treated 100% equally by their managers. So where did the difference in performance come from? One major difference cropped up: managers with more prejudice in the implicit association test interacted noticeably less with the minority group. In other words, they addressed them far fewer times, gave them fewer instructions and less feedback, and kept more distance from the minority group. For this reason, cashiers with North African names were actually less frequently asked for overtime or assigned to cleaning duties.

A greater distance of managers to subordinates has a negative impact on the productivity not only of the minority group but overall. Managers who communicate less with their employees cause lower productivity in their shifts. For companies, this is an expensive problem. Management has a strong impact on business productivity in other respects as well, as Chapter 20 will show.

Takeaways

The relationship between managers and employees influences the working atmosphere as well as productivity. Discriminatory behavior by managers results in a reduced work performance even if discrimination manifests only in the fact that the manager has less contact with certain employees.

References

Glover, D.; Pallais, A.; Pariente, W.: (2017) Discrimination as self-fulfilling prophecy: Evidence from French Grocery Stores. Quarterly Journal of Economics, 132: 1219–1260.

CHAPTER 16

When It's Hot Outside, People Are More Risk Averse and Make Worse Decisions

*P*eople say you should "sleep on it" before making momentous decisions. Less has been said up to now about whether
you shouldn't make important decisions when it's hot outside. That might change soon. In the age of global warming, heat
will become an important decision-making factor, and it would
be smart to take that into account when making far-reaching
decisions.

Global temperatures are rising, and we are going through
one record summer after the next. That global warming has
had, and will have in the future, a dramatic impact on human
beings and the environment is without question. Important
decisions must be made to stop the warming. Decisions are war-
ranted on all levels: at the international level, for example, in
the form of climate agreements; at the national level, in national
climate protection packages; or at the individual level, in relation to individual consumer decisions, which in total contribute
to the ecological footprint of every human being. The increasing warming therefore requires a multitude of momentous
decisions. But ironically, the heat itself can have a significant
influence on human decisions.

Conventional models of human decision-making behavior
completely ignore the factor of heat. According to these models,
referred to as *neoclassical* in economic theory, only the costs and

benefits of specific decisions and the choices they are based upon play a role, while things such as heat, tiredness, or general mood are seen as insignificant. However, psychological research shows that heat reduces general well-being, mood, and a willingness to perform. At higher temperatures, people are less likely to take risks, and they place more trust in previously consumed products and thus in their own habits.

Only in recent years has behavioral economic research addressed the question of whether seemingly insignificant factors such as heat play a role in important professional decisions. You might think that this wouldn't be the case in highly industrialized countries, where more and more offices are air-conditioned and people work at agreeable temperatures even when it is very hot outside. Recent research conducted by Anthony Heyes and Soodeh Saberian of the Canadian University of Ottawa shows that this assumption is erroneous.

Heyes and Saberian checked whether the outside temperature has a measurable impact on the decisions of judges in the United States. To this end, they examined almost 207,000 judicial decisions over applications for immigration to the United States and almost 20,000 decisions on the suspension of a prison sentence for probation. In both cases, the judges' decisions had a very significant and immediate impact on the applicants concerned. The courts where the rulings were made were all air-conditioned, so the judges were protected from the outside heat during their working day. But Heyes and Saberian nonetheless measured the respective outside temperatures (every hour between 6 a.m. and 4 p.m.) and then checked whether the outside temperature had an influence on court decisions.

The result is a resounding yes. With an increase in the outside temperature of 10 degrees Fahrenheit, the probability of a positive decision in an immigration procedure declined by about 6%; in an application for probation, it declined by about 10%. The probability that an immigration application was decided positively declined from 16.4% to 15.3% (a reduction of approximately 6% of the initial 16.4%); in the case of applications for probation, it declined from 16.5% to 14.9%. The statistical analysis took into account other factors such as the normal decision-making behavior of a judge, the nationality of the applicant, or the severity of the crime in the case of a prisoner, but they didn't eliminate the influence of increased temperatures.

The same effects can be observed when you look at daily temperature in comparison to the normal temperature in a given month. Higher temperatures seem to lead to different decisions.

Since the vast majority of decisions in these cases is negative, a decline in positive decisions should be considered as more risk-free. This pattern fits in quite well with psychological research findings, according to which higher temperatures make people more risk-averse and less ready to "swim against the tide." According to psychological research, one of the most influential factors is the general mood that worsens with unusually high temperatures compared to "normal" temperatures. This could explain the tendency toward negative judge decisions. Heat also reduces cognitive performance, according to psychological research, which is likely to play a role as well.

There are other surprising factors that influence the decisions of judges. For example, if the local football team wins big, there are more judges' decisions favorable to the defendants. This again is a question of the predominant mood, in this case, after sports events. But while sports events can turn out good or bad, the development of global temperatures is going in only one direction, namely, upward. This does not make the important decisions for combating climate change any easier.

Takeaways

When weighing the pros and cons of a given decision, external factors such as heat, humidity, and such play no role from a traditional point of view. Such factors have a measurable impact on human decisions, though, since they affect the mood and risk appetite of people.

References

Heyes, A.; Saberian, S.: (2019) Temperature and decisions: Evidence from 207,000 court cases. American Economic Journal: Applied Economics, 11: 238–265.

CHAPTER 17

Managers with Good People Management Skills Increase Employee Satisfaction and Reduce Turnover

*P*eople management skills is a new term in management literature. The capability of supervisors to manage their employees well benefits all: employees, supervisors, and the company as a whole. But what really matters here, and how can it be measured?

In major companies, it is common today for employees to be regularly surveyed about job satisfaction and how they rate supervisors, colleagues, and subordinates. Often people perceive these surveys as time-consuming and boring. But important findings can be derived from the surveys, as can be seen from a case study of an American high-tech company.

The company asks their employees, numbering more than 10,000, at regular intervals about various aspects of their workplace. The assessment of the leadership qualities of the respective supervisors constitutes a key part of the interviews. On a scale from "Strongly disagree" to "Strongly agree," employees are requested to state their degree of agreement with each of the following six questions. The questions relate to the respective supervisors regarding whether they

1. communicate clearly what work performance they expect;
2. offer regular coaching and tips on how somebody can improve their performance;
3. actively promote an employee's career;
4. involve other people in important decisions;
5. create a positive mood on the work team, even at difficult conditions;
6. are people you can trust.

The answers to these six questions are used in the company to measure the people management skills of the respective manager. The focus is not on their general social skills (as described in Chapter 4), but explicitly on their ability to lead the employees under them.

Using this data, Mitchell Hoffman of the University of Toronto and Steven Tadelis from Berkeley analyzed how the leadership skills of managers affect the behavior of subordinates and to what extent these skills pay off for the managers themselves and for the company as a whole. To this end, they established a leadership performance metric for more than 1,000 supervisors (managers) who, on average, were responsible for 10 employees. The metric goes higher the more frequently the subordinates answered with "Agree" or "Strongly agree" to the six questions. Then Hoffman and Tadelis correlated these metrics with the performance and the conduct of the respective subordinates; subsequently, they examined whether the respective metric is an indicator for what the manager's career looks like in the company.

It turns out that the leadership qualities of managers have a strong impact on the job satisfaction of their employees and on how long they stay with the firm. Employees whose managers have better leadership qualities are far more satisfied with their work and are more dedicated to the company according to employee surveys. They also stay with the company longer if their supervisors are better leaders. At this high-tech company, an average of 16% of the workforce departs every year. With the best managers in terms of their leadership skills, this figure drops to 14%—a 10% improvement.

There is one especially vital detail that was investigated for the very first time in Hoffman and Tadelis's work. When employees depart, it can be good or bad for the company. Of course, every business wants to keep good employees for a longer period; in the case of bad employees, companies are glad when they leave. The high-tech company systematically ascertained in its personnel files whether an employee's departure was classified as "regrettable" or "good" for the company. Hoffman and Tadelis were able to show that managers with great leadership qualities mainly reduce the likelihood that good employees leave the company. They reduce the "regrettable" cases. In addition, employees are less likely to seek transfers when they work for managers with great leadership qualities. When employees stay with the company for longer periods and request transfers less frequently, the company saves the expense of hiring new people or of in-house transfers, which can be considerable.

Hoffman and Tadelis didn't find that leadership skills impact work productivity, which may not be surprising in the high-tech industry, where it is difficult to quantify accurately highly qualified work (such as software programming).

For managers themselves, good leadership skills pay off immediately. Managers with the 10% best scores are promoted three times on average more often than managers with the 10% worst scores. They also get larger salary increases. While salary increases of managers are around 4% to 8% per year, those with the best scores for leadership qualities receive another 1.5% more a year. So people management skills are worthwhile, and are so more and more.

Takeaways

Executives today are expected to communicate in a transparent manner what is expected when it comes to their employees' work performance, to give regular feedback, to promote their employees' careers, and to provide guidance and advice. People who have these skills are better able to "manage" people, thus reducing employee churn and heightening job satisfaction.

References

Hoffman, M.; Tadelis, S.: (2021) People management skills, employee attrition, and manager rewards: An empirical analysis. Journal of Political Economy, 129: 243–285.

CHAPTER 18

Can You Trust Your Bankers? The Finance Industry Attracts Less-Trustworthy People

*S*ome industries have a good reputation; others, less so. One reason might be the culture prevailing in certain sectors, another the way of selecting staff. Using the example of the financial sector, this can be demonstrated in quite tangible terms.

Peter, a B.A. student at the University of Frankfurt in his last semester, takes part in an experimental study that deals with the question of how trustworthiness can be measured. The rules of the experiment are as follows: One person receives $8 and must decide whether they want to give some of the $8 to a second person. The amount given is tripled. Then the second person can give back part of the threefold amount (which is not tripled again, though). Peter got $24 from the first person, which means the first person has given him the entire $8. Now Peter wonders whether he should reward the trust of the first person—who remains anonymous in the experiment—by sending back a large part of the $24 or if he ought to concentrate on his own wallet and keep (nearly) everything himself. Peter's trustworthiness is the vital aspect here. After he's made his decision, he answers a few questions about his life, for example, which internships he has done during his time at University of Frankfurt and where he'd like to work after graduating.

Peter was one of 268 students who took part in one of my studies, performed in Frankfurt, Germany, as this is *the* financial center of Europe. Together with my co-authors Andrej Gill, Matthias Heinz, and Heiner Schumacher, I investigated the question of whether the trustworthiness of participants in our experiment was related to the question of where they wanted to work after graduation. The more specific question was whether participants who wanted to work in the financial sector are less trustworthy than participants who wanted to earn their money elsewhere. Given the financial crisis and the dubious business practices of many banks during the crisis, the financial sector is plagued by an image problem and a loss of trust. In Chapter 46, I'll look into the question of whether this has something to do with the dominant corporate culture there. At this point, though, we want to find out whether less trustworthy people seek to work in this industry. Then the problems that finance has with trust would be largely due to negative self-selection.

Why is trust so vital to the financial industry? Customers—from small-scale savers to companies that have to fund their investments—generally know far less about optimal investment strategies and the advantages and disadvantages of various financial products than investment experts do. The result is that customers greatly depend on the trustworthiness of their consultants.

The experiment described had the aim of measuring the degree of trustworthiness of our study participants. Then we investigated whether this degree was related to the industry in which a participant wanted to work after graduation. We divided our participants into two groups: one with a great deal of interest in a career in the financial industry; and a second group of people who had no or only a little interest in it. As it turned out, participants with a high level of interest on average sent back 25% less money in the role of Peter than participants who were not seeking a job in the financial sector.

Since intentions voiced during studies are not yet an indication of the industry in which someone will work after obtaining their degree, we contacted all the participants again about six years subsequent to our experiment and gathered information about their professional career. Remarkably, we found the same pattern. Those who actually worked in the financial sector after graduation had sent back approximately 20% less when playing the second person in our experiment than those who started their career in another industry.

These differences suggest a systematic self-selection of students who enter the financial sector. This was also confirmed in a second study, in which we found that students with a greater interest in the financial industry were less cooperative and more selfish in a cooperation experiment we carried out. Yet another study showed that such behavior does not come as a surprise to other people. We asked other students in Frankfurt how much money—in the role of the first person (earmarked for receiving $8)—they wanted to send to participants in the experiment described previously, conditional on whether those other participants wanted to work in the financial sector or aimed for a career in a different segment of the economy. It became apparent that participants wanting to work in the financial sector were trusted less. On average, they received 10% less from the first person. This fits well with the fact that people who see their future in the financial sector are less trustworthy.

One part of our study dealt with the recruitment criteria stated in job ads in the financial sector. We examined the ads and conducted interviews with HR managers. Analytical skills played a prominent role in hiring. Cooperation and trustworthiness, by contrast, were practically irrelevant and were not stated as criteria or reviewed in any way. This is definitely not conducive to public trust in the finance industry and raises the question of whether different recruitment strategies wouldn't be more beneficial in the long term.

Takeaways

In many industries, customers know less about the products sold and their quality than the company selling them. This is why the trustworthiness of employees plays a crucial role in the public perception of an industry, and hiring procedures should take this into account.

References

Gill, A.; Heinz, M.; Schumacher, H.; Sutter, M.: (2022) Trustworthiness in the financial industry. Management Science, in press.

CHAPTER 19

Peer Pressure Productivity: Employees Are Influenced by the Productivity of Others Around Them

A *company's success depends on the motivation of employees to do their work quickly and thoroughly. In the case of fixed wages, there may be incentives not to make too much of an effort to maintain an easy work life. Social norms help to keep productivity high even in such cases.*

"At last, the weekend!" Caroline thinks. She just needs to do some shopping at the supermarket for the weekend, and then she'll enjoy the afternoon with friends outdoors. At the supermarket she has collected all she needs and is pushing her shopping cart to the checkout. As always on Saturdays, the lines are fairly long. She chooses the seemingly shortest line in front of a checkout with a young cashier. Progress is pretty slow. Customers at the other checkouts are processed much faster. This isn't the first time something like this has happened to Caroline. Once more, she is annoyed at herself for choosing the wrong checkout. Apart from her seeing herself as an eternally unlucky person, she asks herself why the various cashiers cannot be equally fast and if their working speed could be increased.

The manager of the supermarket asks herself the same questions. How work productivity can be boosted is something fundamental to businesses. But it's quite natural that not all employees are equally productive. However, there might be ways to increase the productivity of individual employees. Whether and why such a thing can succeed is also a major topic in behavioral economic research on organizations.

Alexandre Mas and Enrico Moretti of the University of California, Berkeley, analyzed the data of a major Italian supermarket chain. They examined the performance of cashiers. To this end, they ascertained the number of scanned products in 10-minute intervals for 394 people who worked at one of the supermarket checkouts from 2003 to 2006. For each interval, it was known exactly who was operating which particular checkout. As is common at many supermarkets, the cashiers are seated perpendicular to the belt conveying the goods and the customer line. This means that the person seated behind checkout 1 at the very left can view in a straight line checkouts 2 and 3 and so on. Although the person at checkout 1 only sees the back of the cashier seated in front of them, they can see how fast the cashier is working. The cashier at checkout 2 has her back toward checkout 1, so she cannot see it unless she turned around, which she cannot do in front of waiting customers. However, she can see checkouts 3 and 4 and so on, until the last cashier who has her back toward all other checkouts and cannot see the speed of the cashiers there.

Could it be that it is relevant to productivity where somebody sits in this work environment? At first glance, you might think everybody works as fast as they can, regardless of who is behind or in front of them. But that's not true. The study by Mas and Moretti clearly shows that the order in which the cashiers are sitting and whom they have in their field of vision plays a role. For it to play a role at all, it is assumed that not all cashiers work at the same speed, that is, do not scan the same number of products per minute. The 10% cashiers who were the quickest were 30% faster than the slowest 10% of cashiers. The productivity of a cashier depended heavily on who was seated behind them but not on the person they could see in front of them. Let's assume the fastest cashier sits at checkout 1 and sees cashier 2 in front of them. Cashier 2 thus knows that her speed can be directly observed by cashier 1. Mas and Moretti's estimates suggest that cashier 2 works almost 2% faster than usual if cashier 1 behind her is 10% faster than herself. Having a productive employee behind a cashier makes the cashier faster—not equally fast because there are differences between individuals, but the speed and thus the productivity are converging. Intriguingly, the speed of cashiers 3 and 4 has no effect on the productivity of cashier 2 because they can't observe cashier 2. The productivity of cashiers 3 and 4, in turn, depends on that of cashier 2, though. The impact declines the farther away a cashier sits. The productivity of cashier 10, for instance, no longer depends on the speed of cashier 1, even if cashier 1 can still see cashier 10.

What's the meaning of these correlations? If productive employees are positioned such that they can observe you, this exercises social control. Then it's more difficult to make less of an effort and shift the workload to others. The productive employee would directly perceive such behavior, and this is why the cashier who's being watched works harder. In the study by Mas and Moretti, this impact was stable throughout the three years that were observed. The downside is that productivity declines if a cashier can be watched by a less productive cashier. Then it appears more acceptable to people not to make the usual effort. The arrangement of employees in such an environment is of massive significance for the productivity of companies.

In economics, this phenomenon is referred to as the *peer effect*, that is, the influence of people in close (social) proximity on the behavior of others. The effect doesn't occur only in businesses but also in schools and universities. The better the classmates or fellow students are, the better your own grades are. This, in turn, is a stepping stone toward a successful career, so you'd better surround yourself with skilled and productive peers.

Takeaways

Social norms influence human decision-making in every situation of life. Something perceived as appropriate behavior rubs off on other people's own behavior. This is true in professional life as well. It's of relevance in this context whether one's own behavior can be observed. If this is the case, your work performance adapts to those peers who can observe you.

References

Mas, A.; Moretti, E.: (2009) Peers at work. American Economic Review, 99: 112–145.

CHAPTER 20

Employees Who Don't Support the Company Mission Are 50% Less Productive Employees

*A*lmost all companies today have a *"mission statement,"* in other words, a description of their goals. The mission statement is to signal both internally and externally what the company stands for and what values it embodies. Do people work better if they identify with these goals and values?

Deutsche Bahn likes to boast it's a leading global mobility service provider that places great value on comfort and punctuality. As a long-standing customer, I always have to smile slightly at the hifalutin standards of the railway company. For me, it would be enough if the train I use for my weekly commute between Austria and Germany would arrive at its destination on time (something that has been less and less the case over the last few years). The company's mission doesn't match customers' perception at all. Employees of Deutsche Bahn likely think the same thing. When the official goals of a company repeatedly clash with reality, employees will find it increasingly difficult to identify personally with the corporate goals. Of course, this is not just true of Deutsche Bahn but of all companies.

Businesses have a legitimate interest in ensuring that their employees take a positive attitude toward their respective company's goals and values because it leads to greater commitment and better performance. First off, companies hope for a boost in job satisfaction. And beyond that, they trust it will increase productivity. A corporate mission that is accepted and supported by the workforce doesn't only send a signal to customers about what the company stands for—it also yields an immediate economic benefit. However, measuring and quantifying this benefit in conditions that are undistorted is a research challenge that has important practical implications. Businesses need to know whether approval of their mission is significant because it can have direct consequences for the recruitment of personnel.

Jeffrey Carpenter of Middlebury College in Vermont came up with a brilliant idea for how to measure whether the employees' approval of their company's mission actually affects productivity. To do so, Carpenter conducted the following study two months prior to the presidential election in 2012: students who were interested in a minor side job were asked by the makers of the study about their political attitude and their opinion on Barack Obama, the Democratic incumbent, and Mitt Romney, the Republican challenger. The students were requested to answer questions about whose positions in the election campaign seemed more attractive to them, whom they would vote for, and whether they're registered voters of one of the parties.

A few weeks before the election, the students were offered a job for a brief period. They were asked to send letters for one of the two candidates to voters in Ohio, a highly contested state. Who was to write and send a letter for which candidate was randomly assigned. This meant that some participants worked for the candidate they supported; others were asked to campaign for the candidate they rejected. This meant that some were able to identify with their "employer," while others had opposing views.

Carpenter was able to show that the work performance was about 70% higher if a study participant was allowed to work for their preferred candidate, that is, approved of the candidate's (political) mission. Higher productivity included working faster and making fewer mistakes. Someone who had to work for a candidate they didn't like worked more than 40% less than others who had a completely neutral position toward both candidates. Obama supporters who had to send out letters for Romney worked about 50% less productively than an Obama supporter who dispatched letters for Obama. Romney supporters were likewise twice as productive when working for their candidate and not for Obama.

Identification with the employer's goals is of great relevance to the motivation of employees. A wide discrepancy between commercial goals and employee attitudes, by contrast, reduces productivity.

Carpenter also concentrated on the question of whether motivation can be "bought" to a certain extent if employees don't agree with the goals of the employer. Some participants in his study received a fixed remuneration, regardless of their productivity. In this case, the results described earlier were attained. Another group of participants got more money the more work they performed. It turned out that students who worked for "their" candidate increased their output only marginally when getting extra money. Identification with the candidate's goals was obviously sufficient motivation to work hard. The situation presented itself quite differently for students who had to work for the candidate they rejected. Given extra money for better performance, their output notably increased. The difference between them and the group of students who agreed with their candidate declined by about 50% compared with the situation with fixed pay.

Financial incentives can at least reduce but not remove completely the discrepancy between the goals and attitudes of employees and companies and thus lacking motivation. When employees agree with the mission statement of their employer, work seems a lot less arduous, and productivity is measurably higher. These findings show once more just how important personnel selection is because it pays off if employees can identify with a company's mission.

Takeaways

> More and more companies are committing to a defined mission and creating a catalog of values to which they pledge themselves. But if the people working there cannot identify with the mission, work performance is impeded owing to a lack of motivation.

References

Carpenter, J.; Gong, E.: (2016) Motivating agents: How much does the mission matter? Journal of Labor Economics, 34: 211–236.

CHAPTER 21

The More Collaborative Your Team Members, the More Fish You Will Catch

*C*apacity for teamwork is one of the most frequent requirements expected from applicants in job ads. This is because
in many companies, work is organized in teams. But can
you measure cooperation?

The sea is rough, but the helmsman Shinji, a 60-year-old
Japanese man, heads the boat unerringly for the best fishing
grounds. As always, the day's goal is to get as many fish as possible out of Toyama Bay on the west coast of Japan, and then
sell them on the local market and to large retail chains. Shinji is
working together with eight other men—five on the large fishing
boat, who are responsible for the nets and hauling in the fish;
and three on land, who repair other nets while the boat is away
and take care of contact with the retail chains. One special feature of Shinji's team is that the total fish catch is divided equally
among all team members. All are equal partners, even if, as the
helmsman Shinji determines the course of the boat alone. Many
such teams work in Toyama Bay: several people work together
and share the catch on equal terms. Shinji is quite pleased with
his colleagues on the team, most of whom he has known for
many years. Everybody helps the next guy and is willing to step
in when a colleague doesn't feel so great that day. Shinji knows
that this is not the case on all teams. On other boats, arguments

involving whether each team member has done his fair share in getting the overall catch are more frequent.

Economic research on teamwork recognized quite early that teamwork has its bright and its dark sides. A key advantage of teamwork is that people with different skills are brought together, and each person can specialize in the things they excel in. This is called gain in efficiency by means of division of labor, an idea harking back to David Ricardo in the early 19th century.

One major disadvantage of teamwork—compared to individuals working alone on a specific task—is that teams tend to attract "freeloaders." This means that one team member is lazy at the expense of others; he works less and doesn't give his best. When the returns of teamwork, for example, the day's catch of fish, are divided equally among all team members, it unfortunately provides an incentive to every member to reduce their own effort: "I'll take it easy; let the others work like dogs." The lazy ones get to enjoy the fruits of the work of others. And when everybody thinks in this way, nobody is motivated any longer, and the productivity of the team declines. As a result, everyone is worse off. If, for example, the workers who haul in the nets on Shinji's boat are dissatisfied with their colleagues who bring the fish to the market and the retail chains, they may reduce their effort, which is a detriment to the whole group of fishermen. In teamwork, it is important that everybody trusts that the other people work for the good of the team because otherwise individuals will reduce their performance. It's called *conditional cooperation*. Somebody commits to the team if he expects and actually perceives that the other team members do the same.

In a study, Jeff Carpenter of Middlebury College in Vermont investigated whether the level of conditional cooperation on a team leads to higher productivity. To do so, he conducted the field study with the Japanese fishermen. First, he measured an individual fisherman's willingness to cooperate. Groups with four people were formed. Then each man was allocated a sum of money that he could either keep for himself or put into the group pot. The sum in the group pot was doubled by the study authors and then distributed equally to all four people. This means that when you put one money unit in the pot, it turns into two units to be distributed in the group, so ultimately each of the four people receives half a unit. If you keep one money unit for yourself, it remains a whole unit—which is more profitable from an individual point of view than putting the money in the pot. So everybody has an incentive to keep the money for themselves and put nothing in the money pot.

The behavior of the fishermen who participated in the study showed, on average, a relatively high degree of cooperation—that is, willingness to put the money in the group pot. However, there were considerable differences between the teams of fishermen who shared their catch with respect to the level of cooperation of its members. These differences were reflected in the actual catches. Those fishing teams caught the most fish whose members on average showed the greatest willingness to cooperate.

Cooperation boosts productivity because it motivates everybody to act in concert and keep an eye on the common good instead of thinking of only their own interests. This is the reason so many job postings emphasize the capacity for teamwork—the capacity for cooperation—as a key hiring requirement and why Shinji is so content with his team members.

Takeaways

Work teams depend on each member making an effort toward the team's success. People cooperate more frequently the more they expect and perceive cooperation from others. This conditional cooperation means that teams with many cooperative members are more successful and productive overall.

References

Carpenter, J.; Seki, E.: (2011) Do social preferences increase productivity? Field experimental evidence from fishermen in Toyama Bay. Economic Inquiry, 49: 612–630.

CHAPTER 22

Empowering Employees Saves Lives: The Co-Determination Bonus

*T*eam collaboration is important in all companies. Unfortunately, teamwork may easily and inadvertently entail freeloading conduct. Good organizations can prevent that, especially if the team members have a say on it.

It's 3 a.m. in a major American city. The emergency room at the
general hospital is extremely busy. A receptionist records the symp-
toms and type of pain of a newly admitted patient and then quickly
assigns the patient to a team of two emergency room doctors. In
earlier years, the receptionist had to decide which of the two doctors should take care of the man. Today, the employee no longer
needs to make this decision. The assignment works differently now.
The patient is brought to the unit of the emergency room medical
team—which is just around the corner—and then one of the two
doctors decides who will treat the emergency patient. As it turned
out, this new way of assigning is a huge benefit to patients. They
don't have to wait so long for treatment without having to accept
reduced quality in medical care, a study by David Chan of Stanford
University has shown. Why is this, and why does the organization
play a crucial role for productivity in this example?

The processes in a company may foster cooperation or en-
courage freeloading behavior causing the team's performance to
suffer owing to a few members who are not committed to joint
success. The opening example of the emergency room in a major

urban hospital illustrates how the organizational form impacts the productivity of teams.

Chan was able to analyze data on the treatment of more than 380,000 emergency room patients over a six-year period. In the beginning, there were two parallel systems of assigning patients to doctors: either via the receptionist or directly by the doctors on the teams of two in the treatment units. By using both systems at the same time, the hospital wanted to investigate which one was better for patients and the hospital. In a sense, the hospital experimented with the organization of a key process.

Assignment by the doctors on the team—instead by the reception-desk staff—yielded better results: treatment time was shortened on average by nearly a half-hour. The shorter treatment periods reduced the waiting times of other emergency patients by nearly the same amount of time and increased the satisfaction of patients, as surveys showed. But the shorter treatment time did not reduce the quality of the treatment, as a comparison of the two assignment systems proved. The following three aspects were taken into account as criteria for treatment quality: the likelihood that an emergency patient died within 30 days after treatment—it was 2% regardless of the assignment system; the likelihood that a patient had to go back into the hospital within 14 days after discharge; and the cost of treatment. There were no differences between the two assignment systems in any of the criteria. Why were the treatment times shorter? Two components of the different organizational processes are decisive here.

Assignment by the medical team allows for a better assessment in the doctors' specialization about particular diseases and deploying that expertise to the benefit of the patient rather than assignment by emergency room staff. The two doctors usually know which one of them has more experience in a specific case or who has special training for a particular illness. But another, surprising component is just as important, as the data of Chan demonstrates. When the assignment was done by the receptionist, the duration of the treatment was longer the more emergency patients were still sitting in the waiting room. In other words, the physicians were slowing down to signal to the emergency room that they were very busy and did not want to have more patients assigned to them. This is an example of the problem with free-loaders discussed in the previous chapter. Intriguingly, this phenomenon—that the duration of treatment increased with the number of patients in the waiting room—did not occur when the physicians divided the patients among themselves.

Co-determination on the distribution of tasks on the team reduced the likelihood of freeloading behavior and contributed to the success of teamwork.

The insight that co-determination increases the willingness to cooperate on teams does not just hold for emergency rooms but is of a much more comprehensive nature. In a joint research project, Martin Kocher, Stefan Haigner, and I had team members involved in a task of cooperation co-determine whether cooperative behavior ought to be rewarded and freeloading get punished. With this form of co-determination, the level of co-operation rose about 30% compared with a situation in which the rules were simply externally imposed. Freeloading declined considerably when each member had a say on the team's organization and the group's rules, something we like to refer to as the *co-determination bonus* for the extent of cooperation.

Takeaways

On work teams, various tasks must be assigned as efficiently as possible to single members to be successful as a team. When all team members have a say on the distribution of the tasks, motivation is heightened, and cooperation is improved.

References

Chan, D.: (2016) Teamwork and moral hazard: Evidence from the emergency department. Journal of Political Economy, 124: 734–770.

Sutter, M.; Haigner, S.; Kocher, M.: (2010) Choosing the stick or the carrot?—Endogenous institutional choice in social dilemma situations. Review of Economic Studies, 77: 1540–1566.

CHAPTER 23

Good Leaders Model the Behavior They Want to See in Others—and Employees Imitate It

*H*ierarchically structured organizations often believe that it's best to direct employee behavior by clear instructions and demands. The behavior of supervisors plays a far greater role because human conduct is often based on imitation.

When I was young, I used to work at my uncle's glazier's shop every summer. Not only did I gain a lot of knowledge about installing glass and other practical things, I also learned from my uncle how to lead employees. My uncle was usually the first to arrive on the company premises; he lent a hand in finishing a difficult job even if others could have done it. As the boss and founder of the company, he had authority. He had the last word on important decisions but also exemplified what he expected of his employees: commitment to the company and cooperation among colleagues. Sometimes I went on long hikes with my uncle, and he told me stories about his company. One thing stuck in my mind: "Yes, there are some people I have to tell time and again what exactly they should do. They're probably most willing to do it if they see I don't think myself too good to lend a hand myself or help out on a machine or with an assembly."

The general principle is that good leaders set a good example that employees are willing to follow. Famous personalities in history knew this. Albert Schweitzer, winner of the Nobel Peace Prize, summed it up: "Setting an example is leadership." This knowledge is important for modern organizations because setting an example can be a tool in many ways to direct how employees should act for things that cannot be easily ordered or instructed.

Leading by role model works in a wide variety of situations: the glazier's shop where the boss lends a hand himself; a research institute where the director herself decorates the room for the Christmas party and brings food; or in police work, as a study conducted by Richard Johnson of the University of Toledo in Ohio shows.

Johnson examined the behavior of police officers on patrol. He analyzed the data from two U.S. police precincts where the activities of police officers on patrol were collected electronically. A decisive factor for the research was that the activities of the officers' immediate higher-ups were also known. These higher-ups in rank also went on patrol (albeit less frequently). The time of a patrol duty can be shaped in many different ways. Johnson was interested in whether the behavior of ordinary police officers mirrors that of their higher-ups. That is not to be taken for granted since the rules for patrol duty are relatively vague ("maintaining public order"; "intervention in cases of suspicion"), and officers can only be warned in the event of gross negligence and errors. So it isn't easy to direct the activities of these officers. However, proactive deployment, for example, checking problematic areas more often or seeking contact with citizens, would be desirable in the eyes of many supervisors. Since ordinary officers also have electronic access to the activity records of their supervisors, it can be checked whether the supervisor's conduct has an impact on the activities of the ordinary officers.

Johnson investigated about 1,400 patrol beats in two U.S. police precincts and found that the activities of the higher-ups had a significant impact on the activities profile of ordinary police officers. When immediate supervisors are proactive on duty, the likelihood doubles for their subordinate police officers to do the same. The result is remarkable because immediate supervisors have few options to sanction and direct their officers and because the regulations governing the design of the patrol beat give the officers a great deal of leeway. This leeway also applies to supervisors. If supervisors use this freedom in a certain way—for example, proactive deployment—it increases the readiness of their subordinates to follow this pattern of activity.

The underlying behavior pattern is widespread: people often adapt to the behavior of others in a social context. Leading by role model works because of this behavior pattern, but it also demands that supervisors demonstrate the conduct themselves that they expect of others on their team.

So when my uncle helped with an assembly or was the first to come to the office early in the morning, this meant leadership by way of role model, and his employees gladly emulated him. The downside of this knowledge is that setting a bad example— for example, being too good for lowly work—has a negative impact on subordinates' commitment to work as well as their motivation.

Takeaways

People imitate the behavior of others who are important in their lives. This tendency for imitation makes leadership in a company crucial. If executives don't just talk the talk but walk the walk, employees will do the same.

References

Johnson, R.: (2015) Leading by example: Supervisor modeling and officer-initiated activities. Police Quarterly, 18: 223–243.

CHAPTER 24

Selfish Leaders End Up with Selfish Followers

*H*uman beings are social beings who have the potential and
capacity for cooperation—working together for mutual
benefit—even if the people involved are strangers to one another. In the animal kingdom, this occurs only among genetically
related animals. Human beings can do better. It's vital, though, for
someone to set a good example.

When I talk about the value of cooperation and present my
own research on this topic, I like to begin with an old Chinese
parable that illustrates what cooperation is all about. The parable
goes like this:

> *A man and a women wanted to marry. They didn't have
> much money, but they still thought that a lot of people
> should be invited to their wedding. A joy that's shared is
> a joy made double, they reckoned. They decided to have a
> huge wedding feast with many guests. To make it possible,
> they asked all the guests to bring a bottle of wine. There
> will be a big barrel at the entrance into which all the guests
> would pour their wine. This way, everybody will drink
> each other's gift, and everybody will be joyous together and
> celebrate. When the party began, the waiters ran up to the
> big barrel and scooped cups of the wine. Everybody was
> horrified as it turned out that the barrel was filled with
> water. They sat there and stood around petrified when they
> realized what had happened: every individual guest had
> thought, I'll pour in a bottle of water, nobody will notice*

*the difference or taste it: And now they knew that every-
body had had the same thought: Today, I want to party at
the expense of others.*

The parable underscores the problem with cooperation in groups. Every member has a motive to keep their contribution to the group as small as possible (bringing cheap water instead of expensive wine), while hoping that all the others would contribute as much as possible (bringing wine instead of water). When everybody acts the same way, the common good cannot flourish—it will be a pretty sad party. But when every member makes a contribution, everybody benefits—and it will be a fine party with wine (it's unimaginable today that all the guests would simply pour different wines into a big barrel—a nightmare for wine connoisseurs).

The parable of the wedding feast can be applied to many areas of life. Football teams have proven to be more successful if each player does some blocking and defense for the next player to correct the mistakes of others. Research teams conclude their projects successfully when every member takes an active part in the project and doesn't rely on others to perform the difficult work steps. Cooperative business projects are more auspicious when research and development efforts are coordinated. Teams work more smoothly when important information is shared on time. The list is endless. The benefits of cooperation for all involved is easy to see. But still, there are incentives for individuals to act as freeloaders and to make little or no contribution to the common good. What are the conditions for successful cooperation, given such incentives?

I have investigated one particular factor in several research projects. Specifically, I looked into the question of whether cooperation depends on whether one person in the group sets a good example. In terms of methodology, these studies employ the so-called prisoner dilemma. To put it simply, this means a situation in which each individual in a group of several people is better off financially (or in other terms) if they don't cooperate. At the same time, the group would fare best if everybody cooperated 100%. In the Chinese parable, everybody is best served when each guest brings a bottle of wine so everyone can celebrate. But each individual saves the cost of a bottle of wine if they pour water into the barrel.

Does the willingness to cooperate increase when a group member first decides on their contribution—the extent of cooperation—so the others see this member's contribution and then decide for themselves? Let's take the example of the parable: all the wedding guests watch and wait while the first person pours their bottle into the barrel and checks whether it's truly water or wine. Only then do they decide whether they want to provide water or wine.

All my research shows that there is a much higher degree of cooperation in groups if one or several members set a good example. Other group members adapt to the cooperative behavior of others. This "conditional cooperation" has already been illustrated in Chapter 21. It means that people are willing to cooperate when they see or anticipate that others will cooperate as well.

A positive example is especially effective if it's provided voluntarily. Cooperation doesn't work if someone is forced to be cooperative.

Setting a poor example will lead to the erosion of cooperation on teams because nobody wants to be exploited by freeloaders. Of course, supervisors are especially called upon to lead by example here. Their cooperative conduct will be imitated in all likelihood, while self-serving supervisors who are freeloaders often expect cooperation but don't get any from others because the team members contribute as little as possible to the team's success.

Leadership only works by leading by example. In the words of Mahatma Gandhi, "Be the change you wish to see in the world."

Takeaways

Many people cooperate on a team if the other members cooperate as well. This human trait of conditional cooperation makes setting a good example such an important tool to improve the productivity of work teams.

References

Güth, W.; Levati, M. V.; Sutter, M.; van der Heijden, E.: (2007) Leading by example with and without exclusion power in voluntary contribution experiments. Journal of Public Economics, 91: 1023–1042.

Sutter, M.; Rivas, F.: (2014) Leadership, reward, and punishment in sequential public goods experiments. In: van Lange, P.; Rockenbach, B.; Yamagishi, T. (Eds): Reward and Punishment in Social Dilemmas. Oxford University Press, Oxford, 133–160.

PART IV

Behavioral Economic Research on Gender Differences and Unequal Pay: Women Are More Risk Averse (and Men Overestimate Themselves)

CHAPTER 25

An Argument for Gender Quotas in Employment: They Can Help Attract Highly Qualified Women

Research in behavioral economics shows that there are big differences between the genders when it comes to the willingness to compete with others. Why is this, what significance does it have for the labor market, and what does it mean for the divisive discussion about gender quotas?

Rebecca is sitting in front of the screen in a computer lab at her university. She is one of several hundred participants in an academic study that examines the competitive attitudes of men and women. Rebecca's task is to add five two-digit numbers. She has a total of three minutes to complete as many additions (of five double-digit numbers) as possible. No extra help outside of a pencil and paper is allowed. Before Rebecca begins with the task, she must decide how she wants to be paid by the people doing the study. She has two options. In the first option, she will receive $0.50 for every correctly solved addition. In the second option, she will get $1.50 for every correctly solved addition if she, in a group of six, was one of the two best participants with the most correct solutions. The group of six includes three men and three women (among them Rebecca). If Rebecca is not one of the two best people in the second payment option, she won't get any money. Thus, the second option is riskier but also more financially attractive if Rebecca is one of the best. Though Rebecca has always been quite good in math and mental calculations come easy to her, after a brief deliberation, she picks option 1. At least $0.50 per calculation is a sure thing, she ponders. She does 11 additions correctly in the three minutes and gets $5.50.

The situation I have just described is from a study I published in *Science* together with my colleague Loukas Balafoutas. The results we found at the University of Innsbruck match those done at Harvard University by Muriel Niederle from Stanford and her coauthors remarkably well. In our study, we initially examined if there are any differences between men and women when opting for a form of payment. Although men and women were statistically good in equal measure at doing the additions—the men solved 7.50 problems in three minutes on average, the women 7.41 problems in that time—63% of the men chose payment option 2, but only 30% of the women did! Women clearly shied away from competition, while nearly two-thirds of men were willing to compete against others.

This huge difference in willingness to compete with others between men and women has been confirmed by countless studies. The difference can be explained by the consideration that women are more risk-averse and men consistently overestimate themselves. But even if we take these important factors into account, an unexplained something remains that is referred to in academic literature as a "pure" gender difference. As a rule, women dislike competitive situations far more than men do, even though both genders perform equally well under competitive pressure.

Why is this significant? It is still a fact that women earn less on the labor market and are less likely to be promoted to top management or the board than men. Explanations of this have existed for decades, including discrimination against women, interruptions in employment (due to having children), or the difficulties women have in balancing family and work when their partners are not equal in this work. For about 15 years now, another factor has been discussed a great deal in behavioral economics texts, namely, the differences in the willingness to compete between men and women. On the modern labor market, you have to accept competition for attractive positions to have a chance in the first place. But if one of the genders, namely, women, is less willing to take the risk than the other one—even if their performance is equally good objectively—and thus shies away from competition, the other gender, namely, men, will rise more easily.

It is in the interest of every company—and of society as a whole—for the best candidates for vacancies to be found, regardless of gender. There is no ideal way to achieve this objective, but quota policies may be of some help. In our *Science* study, we wanted to examine the impact quota policies might have. To do so, we added a condition that changed slightly the second payment option in our example. Now it was stipulated that the best of three women in a group of six would win in any case ($1.50 per math problem) and that the best of the five remaining people would be the runner-up winner. This rule is in line with a quota system in which one of the two winners must be a woman.

The impact was a lot more positive than I'd expected before starting the study (and resulted in me changing my mind). With this quota system, 53% of the women chose the competition of option 2 (still about 60% of men). The fact that the very best among the women, like Rebecca in our example, opted for competition is of particular import here. The (uninformed) arm-chair argument that people hired because of affirmative-action perform poorly cannot be reconciled in any way with the results of our study—and that of many others. It is therefore high time to start to discuss politically controversial issues such as quotas for women. This includes more knowledge of why willingness to compete with others is important in selecting a major in college or a profession, in what role the family and surrounding culture play, and at what point gender differences take effect. The following chapters will deal with these topics.

Takeaways

Behavioral economists have found that women are usually more reluctant to compete with others, compared to men. This has implications for the careers of the two sexes. Quotas could motivate the best-qualified women to compete, thus improving their chances for advancement. The concern about underqualified "quota women" does not square with the empirical evidence.

References

Balafoutas, L.; Sutter, M.: (2012) Affirmative action policies promote women and do not harm efficiency in the lab. Science, 335: 579–582.

Niederle, M.; Segal C.; Vesterlund, L.: (2013) How costly is diversity? affirmative action in light of gender differences in competitiveness. Management Science, 59: 1–16.

CHAPTER 26

The More Competitive Your Attitude, the Higher Your Lifetime Earnings

*W*illingness to compete with others influences the job training people choose and their major in college. It also has an influence on whether somebody applies for a certain job. Gender differences in the willingness to compete with others therefore impact the choice of profession—and future income.

Muriel Niederle, an economist who teaches at Stanford University, and Lies Vesterlund from the University of Pittsburgh are deemed pioneers when it comes to measuring attitudes toward competition with others. In simple experimental arrangements—such as the one I outlined in the previous chapter and have used for my own studies on the effect of quota policies—they showed that women, on average, are clearly far less ready to engage competitively than men. At the onset of their research about 15 years ago, the studies were still 100% lab studies. The participants were students who, in an experiment lasting about an hour, had to make decisions on the computer on whether they wanted to be paid for each correct solution for a certain task, for example, adding up double-digit numbers, independently of the performance of other test persons or in competition with the others. If they opted for payment in competition, only the best performer was paid; all the others got nothing.

Such experimental research inevitably raises the question of external validity, that is, whether the behavior in the context of a short laboratory experiment also has meaning for behavior outside the lab. In our case, the question is whether gender differences that were detected in laboratory studies conducted by Niederle, Vesterlund, and many others are relevant in real life as well. Recent studies provide proof that they are indeed meaningful in real life since a readiness to compete impacts decisions for training and college majors, and plays a role when applying for job vacancies on the labor market.

In a large-scale study with Dutch high school pupils, Niederle and her coauthors first measured the attitudes toward competition of 15-year-old boys and girls experimentally; afterward, they were able to track the early careers of the young people. Three years before graduating from high school, teenagers in the Netherlands must decide which training program they want to pick for the last three years of school. There are four such programs: Nature and Technology, Nature and Health, Economics and Society, and Culture and Society. The training programs differ in terms of the degree of difficulty in relation to scientific subjects (e.g., math, physics, or chemistry). The chosen field is an excellent indicator for what subjects the graduates will study at a university after graduation from high school. The more science-oriented training programs naturally yield more university graduates in scientific subjects, who will then earn more money on average than graduates less interested in science.

Niederle and her colleagues showed that the willingness to compete is a useful indicator for the choice of training program and thus the later major in college. More competitive young people opted significantly more often for the more science-oriented training programs. This correlation still existed when the school performance of the teenagers, their risk aversion, and their capacity were taken into account in the experimental tasks.

The willingness to compete is vital not only to the educational career, but also for whether someone applies for a specific job vacancy on the labor market. A research team led by John A. List of the University of Chicago ascertained this in a study with more than 9,000 job seekers in 16 major American cities. The authors published job ads for administrative activities where job seekers first had to announce their interest before they were given the exact job description and pay details. Only then could they officially apply for the jobs. This procedural trick allowed the authors to determine how many of those who showed an interest actually applied for a job—depending on the details of payment. In one case, remuneration was offered as a fixed wage; in the second variant, remuneration provided only a low hourly rate, but the wage could be increased by bonus payments if their work performance was better than that of a second person on the job. This type of remuneration thus included a strong competitive component.

List and his co-authors found that the type of remuneration had a strong impact on the likelihood of women and men applying for a job. Compared to the variant of a fixed hourly rate without potential bonus payments, men applied for the job with competition for the bonus payment 55% more often than women. The aversion of women to competition strongly affects the application conduct on the labor market. Feeling fine in a competitive situation can be considered a competitive advantage in training decisions and on the labor market that men have over women. The role families play will be examined in the following chapter.

Takeaways

Willingness to compete with others has an important influence on training and career decisions early in life. More competitive people tend to choose professions where they can earn more money later and are more likely to apply for jobs where competition plays a role.

References

Buser, T.; Niederle, M.; Oosterbeek, H.: (2014) Gender, competitiveness, and career choices. Quarterly Journal of Economics, 129: 1409–1447.

Flory, J.; Leibbrandt, A.; List, J.: (2015) Do competitive workplaces deter female workers? A large-scale natural field experiment on job entry decisions. Review of Economic Studies, 82: 122–155.

Niederle, M.; Vesterlund, L.: (2007) Do women shy away from competition? Do men compete too much? Quarterly Journal of Economics, 122: 1067–1101.

CHAPTER 27

Willingness to Compete Starts by Early Childhood: The Pivotal Role of the Family

*N*umerous studies have shown that women are less willing to compete than men—with consequences for the choice of career and income. But how do such differences emerge, and at what age do they first manifest themselves? The role of the family is all important here.

Sophie likes going to kindergarten. At the age of five she's been at it three years already. She feels at home in her group and is close to many children. Today, some researchers from the University of Innsbruck, led by my colleague Daniela Glätzle-Rützler and myself, are present. Sophie is excited because we play games with her and the other kids. For us, it's an economic research project, but for the children, it's all a fun game. They are supposed to remove all the star-shaped objects out of a large quantity of baskets and put them into a container. There are many different things in each of the baskets, so it's not easy to find all the stars. The game only lasts a minute. The more stars a child removes from the baskets inside of a minute, the more gifts the child can choose from our experiment shop. In a trial run with the kids, so they can understand the task, Sophie proves to be pretty good at fishing out the stars.

Then we explain to Sophie and the other children that they have two ways to play the game. In the first case, the number of gifts they can receive depends solely on how many stars they can pick out of the baskets. This means their reward is independent of the performance of the other kids. In the second case, they can get twice as many gifts if they find more stars than another child (from a different kindergarten group). The reward now depends on whether somebody comes out better than another child. Although Sophie is more skillful than most boys—we had measured it exactly—she opts for the first variant without competition. And so do most of the other girls, while the majority of boys opts for the second variant with competition, though on average they collect substantially fewer stars than the girls do.

Both girls and the boys are quite satisfied with their choices. When questioned, none of the kids answers that they would rather have chosen the other variant.

Daniela Glätzle-Rützler and I were amazed at how early differences in competitive behavior cropped up between boys and girls. In a large study with more than 1,500 boys and girls aged 3 to 18, we found that as early as kindergarten age, girls avoided competition far more often than boys. Numerous studies show that such gender differences exist in adulthood. Daniela Glätzle-Rützler and I were the first to be able to show that they already exist in early childhood and don't go away later.

This raises the question of where these differences originate. One possible explanation is that they are genetic. In Chapter 28 I want to express some doubts about this explanation; nonetheless, a genetic cause cannot be completely ruled out. Another explanation focuses on the family and the formative role models of fathers and mothers. A group of Norwegian economists led by Bertil Tungodden from the Norwegian School of Economics in Bergen investigated the influence family background has on the willingness to compete of boys and girls. They asked a representative group of more than 500 teenagers from 14 to 15 to do a typical competitive experiment; in a second step, they related the behavior of the boys and girls to the income, educational level, and values of their parents.

This competition experiment was comparable to the one Glätzle-Rützler and I conducted in the kindergarten class. The Norwegian teenagers were asked to add up double-digit numbers. They could earn either one Norwegian krone per calculation, regardless of the performance of others, or three Norwegian krone if they performed better than the average of all participants. Tungodden and his colleagues found the usual gender difference in the choice of payment method. 52% of the boys but only 32% of the girls opted for competition. Beyond that, however, they discovered that the family background had a strong influence on these differences. In families with a medium or higher income, the gender differences were quite strong; in low-income families with a lower educational level of the parents, there were no differences, although both boys and girls from these families chose competition far less often.

The most exciting finding resulted from Tungodden's group taking a closer look at the better-off families. The crucial influence came from the father's level of education and professional position. The higher the education, professional position, and income of the fathers, the more competitive their sons were. But the fathers didn't affect the willingness to compete on the part of their daughters. Nor did the mothers. The level of education and professional position of the mothers had no effect on the willingness to compete of their daughters nor that of their sons.

These findings suggest that the role model of professionally successful fathers prompts their sons to emulate them, so they become very competitive. Although Norway is a very egalitarian country in terms of gender equality, the professional role of fathers—who climbed the career ladder through their own willingness to compete—appears to have a crucial influence on the differences between the sexes in their willingness to compete. This is true in a culture in which men tend to have greater influence. It isn't so in other cultures. We'll deal with that in Chapter 28.

Takeaways

Gender differences in the willingness to compete help to explain gender differences existing on the labor markets. But it's not only in adulthood that men and women differ in terms of willingness to compete. The differences are already pronounced in early childhood, are related to children's families, and have very long-term effects.

References

Sutter, M.; Glätzle-Rützler, D.: (2015) Gender differences in the willingness to compete emerge early in life and persist. Management Science, 61: 2339–2354.

Almas, I.; Cappelen, A.; Salvanes, K. G. et al.: (2016) Willingness to compete: Family matters. Management Science, 62: 2149–2162.

CHAPTER 28

Cultural Conditioning Helps Explain Differing Male and Female Attitudes Toward Competition

*C*ompetition is a part of professional life. However, men are usually more willing to compete. The family background plays a crucial role here, but the surrounding culture does as well—sometimes a surprising one.

Until the publication of an important study on the influence of culture on competitive behavior (by Uri Gneezy of the University of San Diego), practically all research on the willingness to compete of men and women found that men much more often sought competition than women. Some thought perhaps the differences could be attributed to the genes. But there are still no reliable studies on how our genes affect our willingness to compete. Others thought culture might be driving competitive behavior. Most cultures are still characterized by the dominant role of males. Men might therefore feel more qualified—and more likely to be called upon by their culture—to face a competitive situation.

If it were possible to find a culture where the understanding of roles is the opposite, where women have assumed the more important and dominant role in society, it could be tested whether the women in such a culture would be more competitive than men. Pondering this, Gneezy and his colleagues set out to find a culture in which women play the more important role. A 100% matriarchal society did not seem to exist, however. But there are matrilineal societies, such as in the northeast of India, for instance, where about one million members of the Khasi people live. In this group, it is always the youngest daughter who inherits the family's wealth and assets (from her mother), and clan membership is defined through the women, not the men. A husband moves in with his wife (even if he still spends some time with his original family), and the wealth and assets acquired over the course of marriage belong to his wife. In this society, the role of women is far more prominent than that of men, which makes it quite different from our Western society.

Gneezy and his colleagues thus expected Khasi women to be more competitive than Khasi men. As always in studies on willingness to compete, participants could choose between payment that is independent of the performance of others and a form of payment where you get money only if you are better than another person in the group. The experiment's task was to toss a tennis ball from a distance of three yards into a trash basket without it bouncing out again. Each participant got 10 tries. In the case of payment without competition, participants were paid 20 Indian rupees for each successful attempt; in the case of payment with competition, they received 60 rupees if they were better than another randomly assigned person. On average, the 80 members of the Khasi people made 2.4 successful tries, that is, the tennis ball stayed in the basket with nearly every fourth toss. Compared to the numerous other studies, it came as a surprise—but not to Uri Gneezy and his colleagues who had suspected it—that the Khasi women were clearly more willing to choose the payment with competition, namely, in 54% of the cases, than the men, who opted for competition in only 39% of the cases.

The study took the people of the Masai in Tanzania as a reference group. The Masai live in a relatively archaic patriarchal society in which women have significantly fewer rights than men and are far less influential. Seventy-five Masai tribe members took part in the experiment, the same as was used for the Khasi people. In this patriarchal society, a well-known picture emerged, namely, that men are far more competitive than women. 52% of the men but only 26% of the women opted for payment with competition. With the Khasi, the ratio was almost the other way around. So culture plays a role.

This is important because culture influences crucial economic preferences—for instance, for competition—and thus steers economic decisions in a certain direction, which, in turn, has an effect on the professional success of men and women.

Takeaways

Our behavior is shaped by the culture in which we grow up and do things. Expectations placed upon the behavior of men and women are also culturally conditioned, and this matters for labor market outcomes.

References

Gneezy, U.; Leonard, K.; List, J.: (2009) Gender differences in competition: Evidence from a matrilineal and a patriarchal society. Econometrica, 77: 1637–1664.

CHAPTER 29

A "Nudge" for Reducing the Male/Female Wage Gap

*A*round the world, men on average earn more money than women. Conventional explanations attribute this to differences in education and interruptions in employment. New findings show there are additionally gender differences when it comes to salary negotiations that result in pay differences.

Every year—usually in early fall—the media reports on Equal Pay Day, which is dedicated to raising awareness of the gender pay gap. Equal Pay Day is supposed to be the day on which you can see how much women earn in a given country as a percentage of the amount men get. This percentage corresponds to the number of days in one year up to the Equal Pay Day divided by the number of days in a year, that is, 365. In the United States, the average annual salary of women amounts to slightly more than 80% of the average annual salary of men. At this general level, though, differences in salary that arise from differences in education, length of career, weekly working hours (full-time or half-time), or the duration of employment interruptions (e.g., for raising children) are not sufficiently taken into account. But even if these factors are considered, women still earn less than men do for the same work and with the identical qualifications. It goes without saying that this conflicts with the idea of justice in the Western world. To be able to change this situation, we need to know more about possible causes of pay differences between the sexes.

Linda Babcock of Carnegie Mellon University and Sara Laschever wrote a very influential book on this subject in 2003, entitled *Women Don't Ask: Negotiation and the Gender Divide.* The book's key message was that men are far more likely to want to negotiate their salary when they are taking a new job; by contrast, women simply accept the salary offered by an employer. Based on interviews with employers and employees, Babcock and Laschever came to the conclusion that men want to negotiate their salaries in job interviews four times more often than women do. People who don't negotiate their salary for their very first job forgo an income of more than $500,000 over the span of their lives. The salary in your first job sets the reference point for the salaries granted by all later employers.

So if you earn less on your first job, you'll have a lifelong disadvantage because all future salaries will on average be lower as well.

The book by Babcock and Laschever—important as their findings were—had the side effect that the pay differences between men and women were to a certain extent attributed to the women themselves: they just don't ask for more. Two questions needed to be asked: is it true that women don't ask, and would certain rules in the recruitment process help in reducing gender differences in negotiating behavior?

A study conducted by Andreas Leibbrandt of Monash University in Australia and John A. List from the University of Chicago provides answers to both questions. The two researchers published job vacancies for administrative activities in several large U.S. cities. Job seekers who were interested initially had to provide their contact data before they received a more detailed job description. Only then could they formally apply. There were two variants of the job description; each applicant saw only one of them. In both variants, the authors of the study offered an hourly wage of $17.60. In the first variant, they explained explicitly that the wage was negotiable; in the second, they dispensed with this additional item and left the question open on whether wages were negotiable. The authors were interested in two aspects. First, does the number of men and women applying for the job depend on whether the wage was described as negotiable? Second, do men and women respond differently in terms of wage demands to the two variants?

Differences did become apparent. If wages aren't described explicitly as negotiable, more men than women apply. The difference is much smaller when the wage is stated as negotiable. Even more crucial is the second finding of Leibbrandt and List. When the wage is described as negotiable, as many women as men ask for a higher wage—for example, by saying they actually expected $20 an hour or that the amount specified was the hourly wage at their last job. In this situation, there is no gender difference in the willingness to ask for a higher wage. To paraphrase Babcock and Laschever: "Women actually do ask." Leibbrandt and List did discover a big difference, though, when no additional information was given that the stated wage of $17.60 was negotiable. In this case, men ask more often for a higher wage than women, and women propose more often than men do that they would work for less than $17.60 an hour.

The results suggest a simple conclusion. If it is clear to men and women on a certain labor market that the wage is negotiable (within limits), no difference in how often men and women negotiate a (higher) wage exists—which could be the first step toward salary equity. Whether men and women are equally successful in negotiations is another question.

Takeaways

Explanations for the fact that men, on average, earn more money than women are numerous and multifold. Some of the gender differences can be attributed to men being more assertive in salary negotiations than women and asking more frequently for a higher salary. But when it's clear that the salary can be negotiated, these gender differences in salary negotiations vanish.

References

Leibbrandt, A.; List, J.: (2015) Do women avoid salary negotiations? Evidence from a large-scale natural field experiment. Management Science, 61: 2016–2024.

Babcock, L.; Laschever, S.: (2003) Women Don't Ask: Negotiation and the Gender Divide. Princeton University Press.

CHAPTER 30

Women Leaders Earn More and Revenue per Employee Goes Up When Women Are on the Board

*T*he vast majority of directors and CEOs are still male the world over. Only around 20% of board members of Russell 1000 companies are female. Here we ask whether more or fewer women sitting on the board plays a role in the range of salaries and in the productivity of employees.

Being appointed to the board is a career highpoint within a company because it says now you've made it. To achieve this goal, qualities as described in Chapter 48 are helpful: on average, board members have better abilities (intellectual and social skills), get things done, have more charisma, and are more strategic in their approach to tasks than employees just below the board level. Board members are much more likely to be male. Even if they have the same qualifications, women are less frequently appointed to a board. But board members and in particular CEOs have a proven impact on the company's success. Does it matter whether women sit on the board?

Luca Flabbi of the University of North Carolina did research on this very issue. Together with his colleagues, he had access to the data of more than 1,000 Italian manufacturing companies. The data contained information on all employees about positions, salary, and gender. In addition, the data set contained information on the productivity in the company, for example, sales revenue per employee.

In the entire manufacturing sector in Italy, the percentage of women in the workforce is just over 25%. Only 3% of all board members are female, and only 2% of all CEOs. Flabbi and his colleagues wanted to know how the proportion of women on the board of directors affects the distribution of salaries as well as the productivity in the companies concerned. They took into account the fact that companies with women on their board had on average fewer employees and lower revenues than those companies in which only men sat on the board. The effect of women on the board can actually be examined by solidly defined methods, especially if you analyze the development within a company in which in some periods there were only men on the board and in others, women as well.

Flabbi's findings show that the salary range changes when women are active on the board, especially when a woman is the chairperson, that is, the CEO. Many previous studies found that women on the board have hardly any influence on the average salary of men and women in the company. Flabbi and his colleagues were the first to consider not only the average salaries in a company but also the whole salary distribution according to gender. They found that well-qualified women in a company benefit from women on the board. Specifically, the salary of women belonging to the top-earning one-quarter of the workforce increases by about 10% when at least one woman is on the board, compared with a situation in which the board is made up solely of men. Men just below the board level earn a few percentage points less when at least one woman sits on the board.

Flabbi and his colleagues attributed this effect on salary distribution to two possible channels. For one, they assumed that women as board members are more capable than men to assess the abilities of women, so they can determine more appropriate salaries (in relation to productivity) for well-qualified women directly below the board level. A second, complementary assumption is that women as board members are more involved in mentoring promising women in the company, thus making career opportunities up the chain of command more accessible to women, which in turn leads to higher salaries.

A second core finding from Flabbi shows that companies with women on the board of directors are more productive. To put a number to it, the revenue per employee increases by 3% when women are on the board. One intriguing result is that this positive effect on productivity is stronger the higher the percentage of women in a company already is. From this, Flabbi and his colleagues deduced something quite astounding. A quota system for the proportion of women on boards as has been discussed in many countries and already introduced in some might have the greatest impact on productivity in those companies with an already high proportion of women.

As we know from Chapter 2, women are often at a disadvantage in recruitment processes—from hiring to an appointment as a CEO. From a social point of view, this is unfair; from an economic point of view, it is a waste of talent; and from a business point of view, it is detrimental in terms of key figures and the survival of startups, for instance.

Takeaways

Although the number of women at the top of companies has been rising slowly, their increasing presence in the C suite has produced impressive results. Women as directors or CEOs influence the salary distribution and productivity in companies.

References

Flabbi, L.; Macis, M.; Moro, A.; Schivardi, F.: (2019) Do female executives make a difference? The impact of female leadership on gender gaps and firm performance. Economic Journal, 129: 2390–2423.

PART V

The Economic Benefits of Fairness and Trust

CHAPTER 31

Trust Is an Economic Asset; Lack of Trust Is Expensive

*T*rust is an important asset, not only in interpersonal relationships but also for the productivity of companies and for the growth of the economy. The economic significance of trust arises from the fact that most contracts are incomplete and do not regulate everything.

What would you answer to the following question? "Generally speaking, would you say you can trust most people or that you cannot be careful enough in dealing with other people?" The question is worded somewhat vaguely. Nonetheless, most people understand the question, and how they answer it has a lot to do with the economy and prosperity.

But first things first. The previous question comes from the World Value Survey that queries attitudes toward social, ethical, or political values in a number of countries. About 25 years ago, Stephen Knack and Philipp Keefer of the World Bank published a journal article that demonstrated the importance of trust as a "soft" production factor. Based on the data from 29 industrialized countries, the authors were able to show that average economic growth was greater in a country the more often its citizens agreed with the World Value Survey statement that, generally, you can trust most people. This result held true even when a number of other crucial variables were taken into account (e.g., educational level or inflation rate). Why is trust important for economic growth and thus prosperity?

Let's look at a few everyday situations. When I went on a hiking tour with my uncle as a young man, he sometimes told me about business partners who were handshake quality. When entering into a deal with these partners, he relied on their word, or the handshake; in other words, he trusted they would keep their part of the deal without signing a contract. He (nearly) always fared well with this principle, and it saved him many rounds of negotiations and legal paperwork. In commercial terms, transaction costs were low, and deals were closed efficiently.

Employment contracts are another example of how important trust is. This may sound surprising at first glance because employment contracts govern the rights and obligations of the two parties and trust doesn't appear to be necessary as an additional component to them. But most employment contracts are incomplete contracts, as economists say. Usually, an employment contract contains basic information—where you work, what your salary is—but the details are missing. In academia, for instance, employment agreements certainly don't specify how you should do your research, how much work you should put into individual projects, or whether you have to present papers at conferences. These components play a major part, though, in the question of how easily research projects can be published and thus affect the reputation of the university. This means that the university trusts you to conduct thorough and academically sophisticated research.

Incomplete contracts appear in other industries as well. The tasks of managing a department, for example, are hard or impossible to demarcate or define in employment contracts because they are too complex and multifaceted. The fact that employment relationships are not regulated down to the last detail constitutes an advance in trust that newly hired employees will perform their duties correctly; second, greater freedom and less regulation heighten work motivation.

Trust is important and makes dealing with one another more efficient, including at companies. What do we know about how trust develops over the course of life? Together with Martin

Kocher, I authored a study on the subject a few years back. We engaged 600 people from Vorarlberg, Tyrol, and Salzburg, between 8 and 88 years old, to participate in a trust game. In this game, the first person is given $10, and they can send any amount to a second person (without provision). Every dollar sent is tripled. The second person then can decide whether they should give part of the tripled amount back to the first person. The returned sum is no longer tripled. If, for instance, the first person sends $10, the second person receives $30 and sends back $15, then both have $15 in the end. But the first person must trust that the second person will give something back. If the first person doesn't trust in the second person, the first person should keep the $10, with the second person getting nothing. The average amount sent is a measure of the trust. Martin Kocher and I discovered that the amount increases almost linearly between the ages of 8 to around 20. The youngest participants sent only $2 on average. With increasing age, this amount increased consistently in adulthood to around $6.60, remained constant throughout adulthood, and declined slightly again with retirees to just over $5.

Trust thus grows over the course of youth, reaches its peak at the beginning of adulthood, and remains fairly constant for a long time. All economic studies show that this is good news because a high level of trust is not just positive in the interpersonal sphere but also for companies and the economic prosperity of a society. Also trustworthiness, how much the second person sends back, increases with age, which is vital for dealing with customers as well as within a company.

Takeaways

In a company, not every work step or every decision of employees can be monitored. This is why trust is so important for efficient collaboration. The level of trust in a society correlates with its economic prosperity.

References

Sutter, M.; Kocher, M.: (2007) Trust and trustworthiness across different age groups. Games and Economic Behavior, 59: 364–382.

Knack, S.; Keefer, P.: (1997) Does social capital have an economic payoff? A cross-country investigation. Quarterly Journal of Economics, 112: 1251–1288.

CHAPTER 32

A Little Accountability Goes a Long Way: Trust Works Best When Monitoring Is Possible but Not Used

M *any activities in a company are subject to broad contractual arrangements. It would be difficult and expensive to regulate and monitor every step of employees in their work. Thus, it's necessary to have trust that employees will perform their duties in the interest of the company. But monitoring has great significance, yet in a surprising way.*

Over the course of my research career, I was lucky that my employers—for example, Innsbruck and Cologne University and the Max Planck Society—always gave me a big advance in trust. Employment contracts didn't govern exactly how much research output was expected of me. Only the extent of my teaching obligation was clearly specified—but only the extent, not the quality of the teaching or how much time I invested in preparation or how quickly I should respond to student inquiries. This means that my employment contract created a great deal of freedom for me to decide on my own how to perform the activities that were required. Of course, this freedom wasn't granted without a certain measure of monitoring by the employer. Various evaluations of my research and teaching activities demanded that I account for past periods. However, I never perceived that as supervision but rather as a legitimate concern on the part of my employer that I use the freedom granted me in a meaningful way (so that, ideally, the reputation of the research institution would benefit from it). The trust placed in me thus created huge incentives to give something back in return to make an effort for the employer, especially since the work conditions were for the most part unsupervised.

If employers are perceived as permanently supervising and monitoring, it can severely impede motivation. But the possibility of monitoring plays a major role when it comes to trust and output. This was shown by two global pioneers in behavioral economics, Ernst Fehr of the University of Zurich and John A. List of the University of Chicago.

Fehr and List examined how an employer's possibilities of supervision impact the motivation of employees. They conducted the study with students and CEOs (from the coffee industry) in Costa Rica. These individuals role-played as either employers or employees in an experimental laboratory study. An "employer" could offer an "employee" a particular wage; the "employee" could provide more or less work output for the money. First, the employers made their remuneration proposal and specified the desired work output—which could be understood as the minimum work output expected. Then the employees were informed of the wage and the desired work output. Based on this, they were to choose their own work output.

Fehr and List introduced two different conditions. One condition, let's call it the "basic condition," exactly matches up with the procedure described in the previous paragraph. The other condition added a small but crucial detail. This other condition—we'll call it the "monitoring condition"—stipulated that the employer chooses whether a certain amount should be deducted from the wage if the employee renders less than the desired output. The employee always knew of this possibility on the part of the employer and was always informed whether the employer was going to make use of this option to reduce their wage. Hence, the monitoring condition allowed for supervision by the employer, but the employer did not have to make use of it. If the employer doesn't, it can be interpreted as a signal of trust to the employee and that the employer doesn't insist on nitpicking supervision.

The results showed clearly that trust is vital; however, the monitoring possibility had an additional positive effect. Specifically, the employees in this study achieved the highest performance under the monitoring condition when the employer waived the possible wage deduction from the outset. Waiving it despite the possibility of monitoring had the strongest effect. The lowest performance was achieved when the employers insisted on the possible wage deduction. Exercising supervision and thus a lower level of trust had a negative effect on the motivation of employees. The performance under the basic condition—when no wage deduction, that is, no supervision, was possible—was exactly in the middle of the two other cases.

There is no easy answer to the question of whether trust is good but supervision is better. Supervision possibilities seem to be helpful if used carefully so as not to send a negative signal to employees.

CEOs were far more aware of this correlation than the students in the Fehr and List study. CEOs waived actual monitoring far more often than the students. It seems that CEOs know better that employees perceive tight monitoring as demotivating. They also know better that a certain amount of monitoring is necessary. Moreover, CEOs are more aware that you have to trust employees. In the experiment, the CEOs offered significantly higher wages than the students did, and the respective employees gave a higher performance. An advance in trust given to employees usually pays off.

Takeaways

A degree of supervision is not harmful to employment relationships. Monitoring mechanisms destroy trust only if they are applied permanently. If monitoring possibilities exist but employers apply them less and give their employees an advance in trust, the mutual trust relationship is strengthened.

References

Fehr, E.; List, J.: (2004) The hidden costs and returns of incentives—
Trust and trustworthiness among CEOs. Journal of the European
Economic Association, 2: 743–771.

CHAPTER 33

Why It's Important to Explain Difficult Employee Decisions: Treating One Employee Unfairly Hurts Everyone's Productivity

*T*he productivity of employees is a key factor for the success of companies. Wage systems often aim at increasing productivity by means of bonus systems or wage increases. It is often overlooked that productivity also depends on how employees are treated. This oversight can be an expensive mistake for a company to make.

Suzanne sits at her desk, a seemingly endless list of phone numbers in front of her and the phone pressed to her ear. She's trying to convince a person on the other end to give an interview. The work in the call center isn't exactly exciting, but at least it pays decently. Suzanne gets a fixed amount, regardless of how many interviews she conducts. That's a good thing because it reduces the work pressure. The working hours are flexible, and the offices are centrally located. Suzanne would have liked to prolong the call center job because she can earn a little money while she is studying. Unfortunately, it will last only for another two days because the interviews will be completed by then.

In a recent research project, I—together with Matthias Heinz, Sabrina Jeworrek, Vanessa Mertins, and Heiner Schumacher—actually leased a call center, hired about 200 people for two half-days, and had them conduct telephone interviews. The study focused on factors that influence the work productivity of employees. Specifically, we were interested in the question of how work productivity is impacted by fair or unfair conduct by the employer. The focus was not on how fair or unfair behavior impacts one employee. That would have been relatively trivial. When an employer treats an employee unfairly, the employee's work productivity is reduced, and intrinsic work motivation declines. That's pretty obvious. We were more interested in the question of whether the productivity of an employee also suffers when their colleagues are treated unfairly by the employer. That's an exciting question because it examines whether fair behavior toward a group of people has an impact on the work output of another group of people.

To go back to the call center: Prior to her second half-day, Suzanne received a message from the employers that, owing to budget constraints, 20% of the existing employees had been randomly selected and dismissed. This message had absolutely no effect on Suzanne herself: her wage (for the second half-day) was fixed; the working conditions remained the same; she didn't know any of the people fired because every individual has their own comfortable office; and after the second half-day of work, she wouldn't be employed by the call center any longer. In other words, the random firing of other employees did not bring any material disadvantages for Suzanne. And yet was the firing of other employees that is perceived as unfair relevant to Suzanne's productivity? Did she conduct fewer interviews after she learned of the dismissal of others? Did she spend less time on the phone?

We terminated jobs deliberately at random. If objectively understandable reasons lead to a termination, it can be communicated. For example, most people consider it fair that the best employees keep their jobs and the worst are fired (this applies mainly to activities for which the performance can be somewhat clearly measured; in our call center, by the number of calls and interviews). Random terminations are seen as unfair, though. Interviews among our call center employees confirm this assessment. Therefore, we were able to investigate whether unfair employer behavior had an impact on the remaining employees. In fact, we found a clearly measurable effect.

Compared with a reference group in which there were no terminations, average productivity declined 11% on the second half-day in the group of employees working (on the first day) the same shift as the 20% of employees who were later randomly fired. In a second reference group, 20% were also given notice of termination, but it wasn't perceived as unfair. Compared with the reference group, productivity in this group remained the same, which means that the unfair firing of others leads to a strong decline in productivity, but justified terminations do not. Employees react to behavior toward others that is seen as unfair.

Other studies have shown that the work productivity of an employee declines approximately 10% if their wage is reduced, that is, if the employee is directly affected by an employer's action. Our results show that a similar loss in productivity may occur if an employee is not affected but observes the unfair behavior by the employer toward colleagues.

Fairness at the workplace is important, and ignoring it may cost the employer dearly.

Takeaways

> People don't care only about themselves. This means that the question of how other people are treated in a company is important for the behavior and work performance of individuals. Unfair behavior by employers has a negative impact on the motivation and productivity of employees, even if they're not directly impacted by the unfair behavior.

References

Heinz, M.; Jeworrek, S.; Mertins, V.; Schumacher, H.; Sutter, M.: (2020) Measuring indirect effects of unfair employer behavior on worker productivity—A field experiment. Economic Journal, 130(632): 2546–2568.

CHAPTER 34

Communicating Good Intentions Gets You a Better Outcome

*M*any companies or public institutions suffer when customers don't pay their bills on time. The administrative costs as well as the effort and expenditure of monitoring can be enormous, so people look for cost-efficient ways to improve the payment morale of customers. One way consists of nudging by appealing to fairness.

Wolfram Rosenberger, himself an outstanding musician, is Director of the Innsbruck Music School. The school educates 3,000 children and adolescents in their free time in various subjects, which includes virtually all instrument genres, choir singing, and folk music. The music school is essentially funded by the city of Innsbruck, but parents are requested to make a financial contribution to the costs because individual lessons account for a large part of musical education and require substantial resources in terms of staff and money. Parents receive an invoice twice a year for a financial contribution to school costs that must be paid within two weeks. Usually, between 40% and 50% of parents pay the bill within the specified deadline. A reminder letter is sent to people who don't make a payment within the two-week period. If there is no response to the reminder, a past-due notice is sent to parents. If the invoice is still unpaid after repeated notices, a music student can be expelled from classes. The reminders and past-due notices entail considerable administrative expenditures, and expulsion from classes as a last resort is done with extreme reluctance since the aim of the music school is to make music accessible to as many children and teenagers as possible and enable them to learn an instrument. It's not in the interest of the music school to enforce the payment deadline by means of harsh sanctions. At the same time, a higher proportion of prompt payments is a huge economic advantage for the school. But how do you get the parents to make punctual payments voluntarily without threatening them with late fees or the expulsion of their children from school and actually execute the threats in the event of late payment?

Companies have to deal with similar questions when confronted with customers who are late on their payments. A tough approach to delays in payment can permanently damage the customer relationship, which is particularly relevant in sectors where customers buy certain goods on a regular basis. Careful consideration must be given to the question of whether a good relationship between the sales staff and customers should be put at risk just to improve payment morale. By contrast, the punctual payment of outstanding invoices is vital to private companies (especially for cash flow) and public institutions, for example, the tax authority in a country that needs to collect the tax debts of citizens. Tax authorities the world over have tried to improve payment morale by means of "nudging."

Nudging means giving people a little push in a certain direction to change their behavior (see Chapter 6). For example, the British tax authority added the following sentence to the notice of tax charges: "We would like to point out to you that nine out of ten citizens pay their tax bills on time." Due to this brief sentence, more recipients of the letter paid their tax bills on time than citizens who received the letter without the sentence. Why is that? First, the inserted sentence reveals a piece of information—how many citizens pay their taxes on time; second, it appeals to a social norm, namely, that it is "normal" and fair to pay your tax bill on time. The appeal to the social norm constitutes the "nudging." People often prefer to opt for those actions chosen by most of the people around them.

My daughter, Charlotte Sutter, who attends several classes at the Innsbruck music school, and Wolfram Rosenberger developed a different type of nudge for the school. The aim was to make parents more aware that they're doing something positive for their child when they pay the school fee. After all, the school fee makes the musical education of their child possible, so it is only fair to pay the financial contribution on time. For some parents, the music school enclosed a yellow slip with the usual invoice (see Figure 34.1), designed by Charlotte Sutter.

This enclosure increased the proportion of on-time payments of the school fee from 48% without the yellow slip to 54% with it—a 12% increase of punctual payments (from the 48% baseline). The positive response was still noticeable six months later. Although no slip was enclosed when the next invoice was sent out about six months later, the payment morale remained higher in the group that had received the yellow slip before (where 52% paid on time) than in the group without the enclosure (47%). Customer relationships based on fairness can have long-term positive effects.

FIGURE 34.1   "Dear parents: Thank you for making it possible that your child is getting a musical education!"

Takeaways

Nudging with appeals to fairness can help establish sound relationships between companies and customers. If communicated properly, the appeals create a positive "tit for tat" spirit that improves payment morale.

References

Sutter, C.; Rosenberger, W.; Sutter, M.: (2020) Nudging with your child's education. A field experiment on collecting municipal dues when enforcement is scant. Economics Letters, 191: 109–116.

PART VI

Salary and Bonuses

CHAPTER 35

Paying People More Doesn't Mean They'll Make Better Decisions

*E*conomic theory generally assumes that higher incentives result in higher commitment and better performance. The assumption is if you pay people enough, they will produce the best results. But if a lot is at stake, it doesn't necessarily improve performance because the pressure can be counterproductive.

Excitedly waiting for the next penalty taker are an audience of 62,500 in Munich's Allianz Arena and about 300 million people worldwide in front of their TV sets. Bastian Schweinsteiger walks from the center circle alone to the penalty spot, puts down the ball, and kicks it into the right corner, but Petr Čech, the goalkeeper for Chelsea, deflects the ball with his fingertips to the right post, and it bounces back onto the field. No goal. Bayern München is at risk of losing the final at home in the 2012 Champions League. At the moment, when everything is at stake, when it comes to making an entire stadium and an entire city happy, Germany's best soccer player loses his cool. And indeed, with the next penalty, Didier Drogba confirms Chelsea's victory and FC Bayern's defeat. A year later, FC Bayern München nonetheless wins the Champions League, but the penalty shootout against FC Chelsea left a wound.

Even before these events, my Bonn-based colleague Thomas Dohmen was able to demonstrate in an empirical study that penalty takers from the home team fail more often than those from the guest team. So Bastian Schweinsteiger's failure was no exception. Dohmen explained this phenomenon with psychological pressure. The positive expectations of the home fans make it seem all the more important to a player of the home team to put the ball in the goal. The psychological burden and the fear of failure increase. As a result, even highly paid top-notch pro athletes who have practiced and performed the activity in question (like kicking a ball into the goal) successfully hundreds of times can fail. So it's not necessarily the case that the performance gets better when there's more at stake.

Traditional economic theory for a long time assumed that better pay leads to better performance and better results and decisions. Good decisions are extremely valuable for a company, for example, when it comes to developing new products, entering new markets, or setting prices in these same markets. Traditionally, it might be assumed that decision-makers make more of an effort and thus arrive at better—and therefore usually more profitable—decisions the more they benefit from such decisions. If managers and directors receive a substantial part of their salary in the form of variable payments, for example, bonuses or distributions, the impact of their decisions on them personally is greater than if they were paid solely fixed wages. The decisions are about more.

Does it ensure better decisions? This question is difficult to answer in a methodologically clear-cut way with field data alone. It is possible, though, in a laboratory experiment.

Dan Ariely, author of several international best-sellers such as *Predictably Irrational: The Hidden Forces That Shape Our Decisions*, conducted a laboratory experiment in India together with his colleagues, in which participants were requested to figure out six different tasks that had to do with logic, creative thinking, and cognitive and physical abilities. In one of the tasks, a helper recited a series of figures and stopped at a random point, and the participant had to repeat the last three figures. Another task tested spatial thinking by having the participant stack nine cubes in a box.

For each task successfully resolved, the participants could earn money. First, they were divided into three groups. The first group could earn a maximum of 24 rupees (4 rupees per task); the second group a maximum of 240 rupees (40 rupees per task); and the third group a maximum of 2,400 rupees (400 rupees per task). These amounts can be illustrated as follows: with 2,400 rupees, an average Indian can pay for goods and services for five months. Accordingly, 240 rupees in the middle condition pay for about 15 days of their expenditures; and the 24 rupees last about one or two days. There is no doubt that the condition offering 400 rupees per task offers enormous incentives to perform well and make good decisions (because who wouldn't want to earn that amount of money in a one-hour lab experiment?). So you might expect the group with the highest incentives to perform the best.

The results point to something else. If you measure success by the percentage of maximum possible earnings the people achieved in the three groups, then a little above one-third (36%) were in the two lower groups (with maximum earnings of 24 and 240 rupees, respectively); only one-fifth (20%) were in the group with the highest possible earnings (2,400 rupees). The same pattern of poorer performance with the highest incentives is corroborated if you look at how often a task was successfully completed in the respective groups. Very high incentives led to more errors in this study. There was no difference between low and medium incentives.

This suggests that moderate (medium) incentives do not yet result in such strong pressure for them to affect good decisions negatively. Very high incentives, by contrast, greatly increased susceptibility to errors. The latter finding indicates that in such situations delegating decisions can be advantageous because a third person may not be so heavily impacted by the consequences of the decisions. Bastian Schweinsteiger didn't have the option of delegating his last kick for Bayern München, though.

Takeaways

> In the past, the idea was widespread that better pay results in better decisions by employees. However, better pay can be a burden and even impede cognitive processes. So decisions don't automatically get any better if more money is paid for good decisions.

References

Ariely, D.; Gneezy, U.; Loewenstein, G.; Mazar, N.: (2009) Large stakes and big mistakes. Review of Economic Studies, 76: 451–469.
Dohmen, T.: (2008) Do professionals choke under pressure. Journal of Economic Behavior and Organization, 65: 636–653.

CHAPTER 36

Team Bonuses Motivate Employees to Work Harder— and to Help Each Other More

When it's impossible or demands too much effort to measure individual work performance, companies like to make bonus payments for the entire team. They're intended to give all team members an incentive to work more and work better. Does it work? This example of a bakery chain provides an answer to the question.

On his way to the office in the morning, Peter, a Frankfurt-based banker, wants to quickly buy a sandwich for his lunch break. He's glad to see the line of customers at the bakery shop is short and he'll be served quickly. He arrives at the office before his boss, who places great value that people in her department start working before she does. Peter noticed for some weeks now that the lines at the bakery shop have become far shorter than in the past. Still, he sees the same faces every morning. So the reason for the shorter lines cannot really be a loss of customers. Nor are there more people working at the shop. And the staff has not been replaced by new people who might be more qualified because Peter has known most of the shop employees ever since he began working for the renowned bank more than a year ago. Without spending more thought on the shorter waiting times, he takes his sandwich, pays for it, and hurries to his bank, where he will certainly arrive before his boss.

My Cologne-based colleague Matthias Heinz, whose research focuses on human resource questions, published with his coauthors a widely noticed study on the influence that incentive systems have on the productivity in a bakery chain. After German food retailers Aldi and Lidl opened their own baked-goods counters, the bakery had to grapple with a noticeable loss in sales at their branches in Hessen. New incentives were supposed to boost productivity in individual shops. At the suggestion of Heinz and his colleagues, the bakery chain introduced a team bonus for all employees at half of its 193 branches, initially limited to a period of three months.

Individual bonus payments were out of the question because the work performance of an individual employee of a shop is not easy to quantify. So a team bonus was paid if specific sales targets were achieved in a shop. A bonus of $100 per shop was paid if the monthly sales target was met or overshot by up to 1%. If it was exceeded by 1% to 2%, $150 was paid; by 2% to 3%, $200; by 3% to 4% $250; and as of 4%, the highest bonus of $300 was paid. The bonus was paid to all employees in the shop in proportion to their working hours.

The German bakery was skeptical at first because they feared a team bonus would lead to freeloading behavior. Specifically, the objection was raised that the lazier employees would profit from a team bonus at the expense of their harder-working colleagues. Then the team bonus would lead to a worse working atmosphere because the more industrious people who are responsible for overshooting the sales targets would feel exploited by their lazy colleagues and subsequently reduce their own work output.

These concerns were unfounded. Compared to the 96 branches where no bonus system was introduced, the 97 German shops with the team bonus increased sales by an average of 3%. Although the payment of the team bonus increased the total cost of labor in the German bakery chain by 2.3%, the introduction of the team bonus was highly profitable. For each dollar paid as a bonus, a shop generated $3.80 more revenue and about $2.10 more profit. Starting the bonus program had paid off commercially—so much so that the CEO of the German bakery chain extended it to all 193 branches after the three-month trial period.

Why did the team bonus have such a positive impact? Surveys among the staff in shops with or without bonuses didn't reveal differences in job satisfaction. "Undercover" shoppers didn't detect any differences in the friendliness of shop assistants or in the frequency with which employees asked afterward if they might get the customer anything else. More detailed surveys showed that the higher productivity was owing to a substantially improved collaboration. After the introduction of the team bonus, it happened more often that one employee handed out the donuts and rolls while a second colleague operated the cash register, so the sales process accelerated. When there was a lull, the time was used to clean the coffee machine and the oven, or else more sandwiches were prepared so they would be ready for the next customer rush, for example, at lunch.

Thanks to the team bonus, all team members acted more in concert and coordinated their work steps more efficiently. This paid off for the employees because they got a bonus, for customers because waiting times were shorter, and for the company because it jacked up profits.

Takeaways

If the contribution of individual team members to the output of the entire team is hard to measure, companies can introduce a team bonus. It improves the performance of the entire team because work processes are coordinated better and productivity is increased.

References

Friebel, G.; Heinz, M.; Krüger, M.; Zubanov, N.: (2017) Team incentives and performance: Evidence from a retail chain. American Economic Review, 107: 2168–2203.

CHAPTER 37

Nobody Wants to Be Below Average; How Performance Bonuses Can Hurt Productivity and Job Satisfaction

*M*any *companies pay bonuses to members of their workforce to reward them for services rendered or as an incentive for their work going forward. When designing a bonus system, several things can go wrong.*

More than one-half of the world's 500 top-earning companies globally use relative remuneration systems. This means that employees get a base salary and on top of it are entitled to bonus payments. The bonuses depend on the performance of one worker compared to others. The bonuses are intended to reward employees for good performance; at the same time, they provide an incentive for a high level of work commitment in the future.

Quite a few things can go wrong, though, when designing relative remuneration systems, as a study by my Cologne-based colleagues Axel Ockenfels, Dirk Sliwka, and Peter Werner reveals. The three authors had the opportunity to analyze the data of a multinational corporation related to bonus payments in locations in the United States and in Germany. In both countries, managers are rewarded by bonus payments, whose amount depends on their supervisor's performance reviews. The bonus scheme has the same structure in both countries but differs in a crucial detail regarding the last step in determining the amount of the bonus.

In a first step, the people in one department are evaluated by their managers on a five-tier scale. The scale covers the ratings of "Excellent," "Above average," "Meets expectations," "Below average," and "Inadequate." The corporation specifies the percentage of managers put in each category. In the best category of "Excellent," there should be fewer than 5%; in the second best, fewer than 25%; around 60% in the "Meets expectations" category; and fewer than 10% in the "Inadequate" rating.

Based on the assessments, the bonus payments are then allocated in a second step according to the following rules. Each supervisor receives a fixed amount earmarked for bonus payments to be completely distributed among the managers in their respective department. The amount of the bonus depends on how many bonus points someone has been given. These points depend on the performance review in the first step, namely, as follows:

"Excellent": 140% to 160%

"Above average": 110% to 140%

"Meets expectations": 80% to 110%

"Below average": 30% to 80%

"Inadequate": 0%

It is a zero-sum game. The average assessment of all managers in the department must be 100%. If someone is given an extra bonus percentage point, this point must be subtracted from another person.

Up to this juncture, the two remuneration systems are identical in both countries. Now comes the difference: for transparency reasons, managers in Germany learn about the bonus points given them. In the United States, by contrast, the managers are only informed of their absolute bonus payment. Since neither in the United States nor in Germany is the fixed amount for the bonus payments divulged (although in Germany it can be calculated by the individual managers), somebody in the United States cannot find out their own bonus points.

Bonus payments account for a significant part of the annual salary in both countries, namely, almost 20% of the annual base salary. However, in the study period, the German variant had a significant negative impact on job satisfaction and on work performance in the following year. Why? This effect was mainly due to the approximately 60% of managers who were assessed with "Meets expectations" and received between 80% and 110% bonus points. If these managers got bonus points above 100%, it did not affect their job satisfaction. But if the bonus points were even slightly below 100%, job satisfaction fell sharply. The same effect could be observed regarding the performance in the following year. Managers who received even slightly less than 100% bonus points reduced their work performance drastically, while overshooting 100% did not have any influence. In the United States, by contrast, where the bonus points aren't divulged, there was no correlation between absolute bonus payment and job satisfaction and/or performance.

What went awry at the corporation's German locations? Two comments from managers illustrate what the problem was:

- "Good managers don't care much about losing a few hundred dollars if they fall below 100% bonus points in the 'Meets expectations' category; but they feel hurt and like an 'underperformer' if they aren't given 100%."
- "The expectation of every manager in the 'Meets expectations' category is 100%. Every percentage point less is a big disappointment."

Nobody who meets expectations wants to be evaluated below average, that is, under 100%. One hundred percent is the reference point. Violating this reference point has a strong impact on both job satisfaction and performance. The point of reference could be established only after the bonus points were disclosed in Germany—with unexpected side effects. So the devil is in the details if you use relative remuneration systems.

Takeaways

Bonus payments are designed to motivate people to perform better. However, it can backfire if the bonus payments violate reference points for what is considered a just allotment of bonuses. They can then have a negative impact on job satisfaction and productivity.

References

Ockenfels, A.; Sliwka, D.; Werner, P.: (2015) Bonus payments and reference point violations. Management Science, 61: 1496–1513.

CHAPTER 38

The Limits of Homo Economicus: Employees Underperform If Their Performance-Based Bonus Hurts Their Colleagues' Bonus

*C*lassical economics assumes that employees work better if the amount of their remuneration depends on whether they render a better performance than their colleagues. Modern behavioral economics shows that belief in the effects of relative pay can be a costly mistake when considerations of fairness come into play.

Francisco has been picking apples since early in the morning. After eight hours on the apple orchard, his back hurts. Working alongside him in his row is Antonio, whom Francisco saw for the first time today although Antonio has been working as a harvest hand on the huge orchard for a couple of weeks. Antonio works fast. In the next row, Francisco sees his friend Pedro, with whom he shares accommodations and who has a bad cold, so he cannot work so fast today. Next to Pedro there are faces he doesn't know. Each worker can see how quickly the other one fills his basket and how often during the day a worker carries his basket to the collecting point. There, the apples a worker has picked are weighed.

The daily earnings are based on the total weight of apples harvested by the worker on this particular day. The company running the apple orchard pays workers according to their relative performance. This means that the harvesting output of one worker is initially divided by the average output of all workers on the apple orchard. The lower the resulting coefficient, the fewer dollars per kilogram of apples a worker is paid on that day. A very productive worker thus pushes down the average pay per kilogram for the other workers. This is because a very productive worker increases the average output and thus reduces the coefficient (of one person's harvest divided by the average harvest) for all the other workers, so they will earn less per kilogram of apples.

This is why Francisco and his colleagues observe quite closely how fast the others work during the harvest.

Classical economics assumes that employees work better if the amount of their remuneration depends on whether they have a better output than their colleagues. The conventional assumption is that this form of relative remuneration will lead to increased effort and thus higher output because everybody has an incentive to perform above average, resulting in an increase in productivity.

The company must have thought along this lines when it came up with a relative payment scheme for its harvest hands. As an alternative, the company could have simply paid a fixed amount per kilogram of apples, regardless of how much other workers on the apple orchard pick on a given day.

Modern behavioral economics has a more differentiated understanding of the choice of pay schemes than classical economics. As was shown in Chapter 37, relative pay schemes can have undesirable side effects because relative remuneration means that one's own performance has a negative impact on colleagues in the workplace. In classical economics, these negative effects are not taken into account because it's assumed that an employee only looks out for themselves. With this assumption, relative pay schemes may indeed increase productivity. But many people don't conform to the ideas of classical economics.

An important reason for this is that many people actually *do* care about the impact their own actions have on others. For the example of the orchard, this means that individual workers are well aware that an increase in the amount of apples they pick will reduce the wages of the other pickers due to the increase in the average amount harvested. If workers see the negative impact on others as unfair and want to avoid it, they must reduce their output. The consequence of such a reaction might be that productivity, that is, a day's harvest, is reduced by relative remuneration and not, as is assumed in classical economics, increased—in each case compared to a fixed amount being paid per kilogram.

Oriana Bandiera of the London School of Economics, together with colleagues, used the data from an orchard in the United Kingdom to examine whether relative remuneration leads to a higher or lower harvest in comparison to when workers are paid at a fixed amount per kilogram. The company switched from a relative pay scheme to a fixed amount per kilogram because the productivity of the workers had fallen short of expectations. After the switch, productivity rose from five kilograms per hour to almost eight kilograms per hour. It should be noted in this context that the average payment per employee and kilogram remained essentially the same in both payment schemes. With fixed wages, the workers on average did not get more money per harvested kilogram.

How can the lower performance in the case of relative pay be explained? As it turned out, output was lower the more friends and acquaintances a worker had in his field of vision—that is, in the section of the apple orchard for which a group of harvesters had been randomly assembled every morning. The negative effect of the number of friends did not occur when the workers received a fixed pay per kilogram. So it is not the proximity of friends as such that has an impact on productivity, but the negative effect of one's own performance on others if friends are nearby and relative performance pay is used.

The authors of the study call that the influence of social preferences on work productivity. Consideration of others was the reason that a relative remuneration scheme led to considerably lower productivity than the company had expected.

For our example, this means that in the case of relative remuneration, Francisco knows that his friend Pedro will earn less money if he, Francisco, increases his work output. This consequence of his own output makes Francisco slow down. As soon as Francisco and his colleagues are offered a fixed amount per kilogram, their own work output no longer affects the income of others, and everybody can work according to their own speed and their own abilities. Classical economics consistently overlooked the influence of considerations of fairness on workers' output.

Takeaways

Most major companies have relative pay schemes in which a higher output is rewarded with more money. As soon as notions of fairness are violated by such systems, output may go down instead of being increased.

References

Bandiera, O.; Barankay, I.; Rasul, I.: (2005) Social preferences and the response to incentives: Evidence from personnel data. Quarterly Journal of Economics, 100: 917–961.

CHAPTER 39

Wall Street Bonuses Incentivize Unhealthy Risk Taking—and Increase Systemic Risk

*B*onus payments are intended to motivate employees to make an extra effort. Performance-based payments can have unintended side effects, however, because they change the decision-making behavior if employees can receive bonus payments only by making overly risky decisions.

Albeit of ill repute, Jerome Caviel and Nick Leeson are well-known names for this type of conduct in the financial sector. One man, Leeson, caused the bankruptcy of Barings Bank, founded in 1717, owing to excessive speculation and a loss of about $1.4 billion. Compared to this, the major French bank Societe Generale was "lucky" in that the risky speculative transactions of Jerome Caviel, which brought a loss of about EUR 4.8 billion in 2008, didn't result in bankruptcy for the bank. Both cases received a great deal of public attention because they illustrated how risky investment strategies of individual investment bankers may lead to enormous losses and even the ruin of renowned financial institutions. Less attention was paid to the fact that, prior to the discovery of the huge losses, both bankers were seen as hugely successful in their field, earning enormous bonus payments with their deals. Is there a connection between risky investment behavior and bonus payments?

The financial sector is not the only industry in which employees are offered bonuses in addition to a fixed salary, which in many cases depends on corporate success as well as on individual performance. Usually, the individual performance is compared with that of other employees; then the amount of the bonus is assessed depending on the relative performance. Such payments are common in many industries. Most sports players get bonuses if their team wins the league's championship. Managers at car dealerships get bonus payments when more cars are sold. Or the employees working at a bakery chain receive a team bonus when a sales target has been reached, as described in Chapter 36.

Bonus payments provide incentives to improve individual performance and thus the company's bottom line. The fact that it may not be very easy to measure individual performance—what did the substitute goalkeeper contribute to winning the championship, or how many additional cars were actually sold by the CEO?—won't be a subject we'll focus on here. Instead, we want to discuss the question of how bonus payments affect human behavior, especially if the actions of individuals have great leverage effects and thus affect others—like in the financial sector, particularly in investment banking. With up-to-date financial instruments, which are often highly complex, huge amounts of money can be moved around. If bonuses depend on how large these amounts are, it might be an incentive for taking greater risks. That is the issue here, as a recent study on bonus payments shows that was conducted by my Innsbruck-based colleagues Michael Kirchler and Florian Lindner as well as Utz Weitzel from Nijmegen.

Kirchler and colleagues had professional bankers take part in an experiment. In the beginning, the bankers were given a basic amount of money that they could put into a fixed-income (i.e., risk-free) investment or in a risky investment over eight rounds. On average, the risky investment generated a higher return, but could lead to positive or negative earnings in individual rounds. In the basic condition of the study, the bankers were paid after the eight rounds the sum of money they had generated with their basic amount. In a second condition, the bankers were ranked after the eight rounds depending on the amount earned. The individual who had generated the most received a large bonus; second and third place still got substantial amounts; the others, however, were given nothing, just their participation fee. This second condition reflects bonus payments that depend on the relative performance of the individual.

The experiment showed that the bankers consistently put more money in the risky investment in the second condition. This was particularly true of those bankers whose ongoing earnings lagged behind those of others in their comparison group. Because once you're in the rear, only taking higher risks offers you the opportunity to get to the front of the line and receive a bonus payment. Similarly, if you suffered losses, you can escape them more quickly if you take higher risks. This may result in the accumulation of risks and even higher losses as the cases of Jerome Caviel and Nick Leeson dramatically prove.

Bonus payments based on relative performance thus amplify the tendency of taking risks to get bonuses. That's very risky, not only for individual traders, but for entire companies and industries. Control mechanisms are needed. However, the abolition of bonuses alone will hardly prevent people from taking excessive risks, as the study by Kirchler and colleagues demonstrates. In a third condition, the bankers were told at the end of the eight rounds what ranking they achieved with their investments. The payout didn't depend on this ranking but just on the generated profit (as in the basic condition). Surprisingly, the extent of risky investments in this third condition was virtually the same as in the second condition. Apparently no one wanted to look like a bad investor, so the disclosure of the ranking alone had an impact on risk-taking behavior.

As long as people want to be the best, the disclosure of one's own ranking leads to behavior of taking higher risks. This lesson is likely to apply not only to the financial sector.

Takeaways

> When companies use relative pay schemes, they give their employees a strong incentive to take greater risks in their work to outperform others. In extreme cases, this can ruin the whole company.

References

Kirchler, M.; Lindner, F.; Weitzel, U.: (2018) Rankings and risk-taking in the finance industry. Journal of Finance, 73: 2271–2302.

CHAPTER 40

Don't Incentivize Employees to Sabotage Colleagues: The Problems with Relative Performance Bonuses

*I*f only one can win, he or she who comes in second is already the first loser. Many companies rely on relative pay, where the winners get a much bigger slice of the pie than the losers. A world-famous episode from the sports world illustrates that such relative incentive schemes can result in sabotaging competitors—for businesses, such a reaction to incentive schemes can be quite costly.

The feature film *I, Tonya Harding* (2018) is based on the rivalry between two figure skaters, Tonya Harding and Nancy Kerrigan, who battled each other fiercely for the only U.S. starting position in the Olympic Winter Games at Lillehammer in Norway. Only the winner of the national championship would be allowed to start later in Lillehammer. So prior to the national championship, the ex-hubby of Tonya Harding hired a hitman, who injured Nancy Kerrigan on her legs with an iron rod. Kerrigan wasn't able to take part in the national championship. Harding won the championship and started in the Olympics, although it had already been publicized that the attack on Kerrigan had something to do with her. Instead of winning by being the better athlete, Harding won after her rival was injured deliberately.

This well-known and sad episode is not an isolated incident, nor is it restricted to sports. If rewards for the victors are very high, damaging the opponent can be as helpful to winning as boosting your own performance. Damaging a rival who is better so as to carry off the victory trophy may also have a negative impact on the overall performance level, something that should be avoided not only from a moral perspective.

Companies struggle with the problem of high incentives for winners. Many businesses the world over bank on relative incentive schemes. This means that promotions, raises in salary, and bonus payments are made dependent on the relative performance compared to others in the same company. Intentional competition is created among employees for the best and most lucrative positions in the company. The idea behind relative incentive schemes is that they drive existing staff to peak performance.

Since it can be quite tedious to put a great deal of effort in your work and the capacity of everybody reaches a limit at one point, an obvious possibility for scoring better in competition consists of damaging your competitors. Whether it's withholding important information from colleagues, disseminating false or misleading information about your rival's performance, or "misplacing" required tools or documents, such behavior is definitely to the detriment of the company because it diminishes overall performance. From the viewpoint of the saboteur, it's an attractive mode of operation if it heightens their own chances for the next promotion or salary rise.

My friend and colleague at Cologne University, Bernd Irlenbusch, investigated whether the extent of destructive actions against rivals depends on how strongly a relative incentive scheme favors winners over losers. In other words, do acts of sabotage increase in number if the prizes for winners are getting higher and higher, for example, if bonus payments are increased?

Since such a research question is virtually impossible to answer in a real company because no management in the world is willing to cough up data on destructive behavior in response to incentive schemes, Irlenbusch examined his question in a laboratory experiment with 336 participants. The participants were divided into groups of four, consisting of a boss and three employees. The latter competed for a bonus they could win if they were the most productive employee. Instead of investing in their own productivity, they had the option of reducing the performance of the other two by destroying a part of their work, referred to by Irlenbusch as sabotage. It turned out that the level of sabotage increased the higher the bonus for the winner became. Relative incentive schemes thus may provide incentives to destroy the work output of others instead of increasing one's own performance.

Based on this result, Irlenbusch then wanted to find out at what conditions the extent of sabotage could be reduced even if high bonus payments for the winner were in place. It became apparent that communication between the employees lowered the level of sabotage because greater social proximity reduces destructive activities. When people know one another better, they are less likely to act in a destructive way. Irlenbusch also found that labeling destructive activities unambiguously as "sabotage" reduced them. He concluded that ethical guidelines or compliance codes that explicitly address such behavior as undesirable make a positive contribution to the reduction of destructive conduct as a consequence of relative incentive schemes.

Takeaways

Companies depend on people working well together. If individual employees can earn more money if they are considered more productive than others, such relative payment systems create incentives for somebody sabotaging the efforts of others.

References

Harbring, C.; Irlenbusch, B.: (2011) Sabotage in tournaments: Evidence from a laboratory experiment. Management Science, 57: 611–627.

PART VII

Ethics in Companies and on the Markets

CHAPTER 41

Markets Hurt Morality: Government Intervention Can Help

*C*orporate scandals such as the one at Enron or "Dieselgate" at Volkswagen repeatedly raise the question of whether market economies undermine morals at companies due to competition. Is that the case?

As a scholar, I listen to many lectures held by researchers around the world. Normally, listening doesn't involve my emotions much. When I listened to a lecture in the fall of 2012, that was a different story. I had invited Armin Falk from Bonn University to Innsbruck, Austria, for a lecture, and he spoke about a research project on ethical behavior he conducted with Nora Szech. In one experimental condition, the study participants had to decide whether they wanted to waive $10 to save the life of a mouse or whether they wanted to collect the $10 with the consequence that the mouse was euthanized. For participants to be able to imagine better what the euthanization of a mouse entailed, Falk showed a video of the killing process (he didn't make the video himself).

As another experiment condition, the participants didn't have to decide individually whether they wanted to collect the $10 and accept the death of a mouse; in this case, they would act on a market. Nine vendors each had a "mouse" (not literally, but their decisions were relevant to nine mice). Seven buyers didn't have any mice. Now both sides of the market could make proposals on how the $20 should be divided up between one vendor and one buyer. If both sides agreed, the mouse was killed, and the respective vendor or buyer received the agreed-on amount. On average, each participant could get $10 again if both were willing to accept the death of a mouse.

The results of this study were noticed around the world and published in *Science* magazine. While in the first experiment condition, just under 50% chose the $10, almost 80% agreed on the distribution of the $20 between two people under the second condition, the one with the market. So, significantly fewer mice survived on the market. Markets, says Falk, undermine acting morally in comparison to a decision taken alone.

Before we discuss possible causes and various countermeasures, it's important to explain something about the mice, so you, dear reader, won't call the Animal Rescue Center! The mice came from research laboratories of university hospitals. There are millions of them in labs around the world. For some experiments, certain mice are no longer usable due to genetic permutations. Since these mice cannot be released into the wild, they are usually euthanized. Falk made the following arrangement: for each case in which a study participant waived the money, a mouse was rescued and wasn't killed; that is, the mouse was kept in the lab until its natural demise at Falk's expense. This means that, in reality, the decisions of the participants didn't lead to the killing of mice but exactly the opposite. Participants didn't know that, of course.

Back to the question of why acting morally was less notable with a market than when it came to individual decisions. First, responsibility for our own actions becomes blurred in markets. In an individual decision, everybody is responsible for themselves. On the market, there is supply and demand, so a second person is always required to close a deal. Responsibility is watered down. Second, acting on the market appears to push awareness of the product being traded into the background. Striving for a good price remains in the forefront. If you can buy a T-shirt for $4, many people are glad about the super-low price; they forget that the T-shirt may be so cheap because it was produced cheaply with the help of child labor.

Do these explanations mean that acting morally on markets can be strengthened by making vendors and buyers more aware of their responsibility? I looked into this question academically with my colleagues Jürgen Huber, Michael Kirchler, and Matthias Stefan. Like Falk, we had study participants in a market negotiate the distribution of a specific amount of money. If the deal did not come about, we didn't save a mouse but donated a fixed amount to UNICEF for measles vaccinations; 100,000 children die of measles around the world every year, and our donations would make it possible to vaccinate 2,150 children. But if a deal was struck between a vendor and a buyer in our study, there was no donation.

To make participants aware of their responsibility, we invited a doctor to give a lecture on measles and the importance of vaccinations; prior to striking a deal, we reminded each buyer and each vendor of their responsibility and that there would be no donation to protect children if a deal was made. Both interventions had no impact on the frequency with which we were able to donate vaccines. In our study, too, markets—compared to individual decisions—tended to push back on moral behavior. Moral behavior was seen to occur more frequently only when it was possible to sanction people financially if they chose money for themselves instead of making a donation possible. It seems that morality has something to do with costs and benefits, as Chapter 42 will show.

Takeaways

Markets are characterized by high gains in efficiency. Market-based action can make people less ethical than when acting alone. This must be taken into account for both individual companies and society as a whole.

References

Falk, A.; Szech, N.: (2013) Morals and markets. Science, 340: 707–711.
Kirchler, M.; Huber, J.; Stefan, M.; Sutter, M.: (2016) Market design and moral behavior. Management Science, 62: 2615–2625.

CHAPTER 42

Unethical Behavior Rises and Falls with Incentives—Make It Hard for People to Get Rich Doing the Wrong Thing

Saint Augustine stated that every lie—independent of its scope and consequences—constitutes a grave sin. Economists think less in terms of black and white. They weigh the costs and benefits of a certain conduct, for example, deliberate deception.

A business consultant once regaled me with the following tale from his professional life: he worked for a midsize company that was in the midst of negotiations for being taken over by a larger group. The company's management very much wanted to complete the takeover successfully and quickly. But the negotiations bogged down again and again, and the management of the corporation kept everybody on pins and needles awaiting a decision. The entire process was quite protracted, something nobody had expected. The company in the end decided to take a desperate—and immoral—move to change the course of negotiations, utilizing their very last bit of strength. It hired Chinese-born actors who showed up at the company in a luxury car to act as alleged potential buyers. A convenient time for the big show had been set prior so that the negotiating team of the corporation got wind of it. Due to this bluff, a decision was made relatively quickly that was favorable for the midsize company, followed by a binding takeover offer that was gladly accepted.

This anecdote—however reprehensible it may be from a moral point of view because the smaller company's act was clearly deceptive—illustrates that moral standards are put through a wringer when it comes to lots of money. Who can claim they are totally immune from temptations of immoral behavior when it's a matter of gaining an advantage? This raises the question of whether the inclination to immoral behavior depends on the size of the hoped-for advantage—that is, whether people resort to lies and plots if they have a great deal to gain and whether possible costs and disadvantages for the "victims" play a role as well. An answer to this question is relevant to companies because it may indicate under which circumstances problems with immoral behavior might be more likely to occur.

Uri Gneezy of the University of California, San Diego, was the first behavioral economist to address this issue systematically. Gneezy's experiment is seen as paradigmatic for the examination of lying by people. In his experiment, two people have dealings with each other. There are two possible results, but only the first person knows how beneficial each result will be for each person. Take, for example, result A and result B. Result A means the first person receives $50 and the second person $60. With result B, the first person receives $60 and the second person $50, exactly the other way around. Then the first person can send a message to the second person in which the second person is informed about what result is more beneficial to the second person. For example, the first person sends the following message: "Result A is better for you." That would correspond to the truth. But the first person may also write: "Result B is better for you." This would be a lie given the money paid with the two different results. It's important that the second person not know the real payments but needs to decide what result they want after receiving the first person's message. This decision then determines the payouts for both people. If the second person opts for result B, then the first person gets $60; the second person, $50. Even after the choice, the second person does not learn which payouts would have been possible with the other result and how much money the first person has actually received.

In Gneezy' experiment, it's then varied what the payouts look like with both results. In one case, the first person can benefit even more from a lie; in the second case, the second person loses even more money owing to a lie. By varying the outcomes systematically, you can find out whether the likelihood of lying depends on the costs (for the other person) and the benefits (for oneself) of lying.

Gneezy's results, which have been replicated many times, can be summarized as follows: as soon as there is a potential gain, people more quickly resort to a lie; however, given the assumption that the benefit remains the same for the liar but that the damage to the other person becomes greater, people refrain from lying if the damage is quite considerable to the person being lied to. But if push comes to shove, one's own benefit counts far more than potential disadvantages for others.

All in all, this means that moral or immoral conduct is based on the costs and benefits of such behavior. In the context of business, this means that when you lay down guidelines for ethical conduct, you should watch out whether there might be a risk that violations are even more beneficial to individuals and that they are rewarded for immoral actions. In the risk analysis of business processes, incentives for unethical conduct can be identified to counteract such behavior as early as possible.

Takeaways

> Many situations in day-to-day work have a moral dimension. How people balance ethics and financial advantages depends on the consequences their actions have for themselves and for others. The frequency of immoral behavior depends on the costs and benefits of an action.

References

Gneezy, U.: (2005) Deception: The role of consequences. American Economic Review, 95: 384–394.

CHAPTER 43

Small-Scale Cheating Can Lead to Major Corruption: Leaders Should Not Tolerate Minor Ethical Violations

*W*hether it's "Dieselgate" at VW or the falsification of accounts at Enron—criminal conduct in companies is often recognized after it's too late. Often the damage has become so great that it can be rectified only with enormous cost or might even lead immediately to bankruptcy. Why is misconduct detected so late so often? One answer can be found in the fundamental psychology of people.

Claire, who graduated from an elite university in business administration, is poring over the accounts of a company to be audited by her accounting firm. She's proud to have found a job with the renowned law firm in her late 20s, even if her employer expects her not to be too fussy when it comes to working more than 40 hours a week. The path to the top is more likely to be open to employees who work on average 80 hours or more a week. But in light of her above-average six-digit salary, it seems a fair exchange of good work for good money to Claire. At the moment, Claire is brooding over a possible problem. She noticed that the company to be audited has posted a steadily growing number of forward transactions over recent years, while competitors in the same industry experienced more ups and downs. Forward transactions mean that a deal agreed on at a present moment will only be executed at a later date. Returns from such transactions look good on the balance sheet. It's just that Claire finds it unusual that this type of transaction has increased continually, almost linearly, even in years that were not so great for business. After pondering awhile whether everything is in order, Claire tells herself that events in the current audit year look very similar to those of the prior year—and then the statements were confirmed as correct and given an audit certificate. Everything is likely correct this year as well since it looks so much like last year's.

In real life, auditing firms—like the one where the fictitious Claire works—earn a good deal of their money by auditing companies' books for correctness and compliance with legal requirements. Given the complexity of the balance sheets of major and multinational corporations, this is anything but easy. During the audit, major changes from previous years are more noticeable than constant small changes over the years because greater contrasts attract more attention from people than do continuous small changes. People tend to judge current situations by comparing them with past situations. In such a comparison, small changes from the past are more often perceived as normal than major ones. This also accounts for the fact that current actions are more likely approved if they're more similar to past conduct, which had also been approved. It's precisely this tendency of people that makes it difficult to identify misconduct that creeps in little by little. Somebody with fraudulent intent can exploit this tendency when assessing ethically correct or incorrect behavior.

Francesca Gino and Max Bazerman of Harvard Business School have demonstrated this in a widely acclaimed study. They speak of a slippery slope that can lead to immoral or fraudulent behavior being noticed too late or not at all. Their study was about estimating the amount of money in a jar filled with small coins. Participants assumed the role of auditor who had to give an opinion on the estimate. If an auditor judged the estimate to be correct—that is, if it deviated at the most 10% from the real value—the auditor received a portion of the estimated value. This means that auditors had an incentive to accept higher estimates because they could earn more money from it. An estimate deemed as correct was checked in one out of ten cases, and the auditor had to pay a penalty if the estimate turned out to be incorrect. If an auditor judged the estimate to be incorrect from the outset, the auditor didn't earn any money.

The jars with coins always contained around $10 in small coins, plus or minus a few cents. The auditors had to evaluate a whole range of such jars and the associated estimates. Gino and Bazerman divided the auditors into two groups. In the first group, the estimates increased by an average of 40 cents for each jar; in the second group, the estimates initially were always around $10 and then suddenly jumped to around $14. Given the rule that an estimate was seen as correct if it oscillated within 10% of its true value, all estimates above $11 would have had to be judged as incorrect. Gino and Bazerman then looked at how often estimates were considered correct that reached $14 for the first time. In the group with the sudden jump from $10 to $14, it occurred in less than 3% of the cases. By contrast, in the other group where the estimates gradually increased, more than 25% of the auditors assessed an estimate of over $14 as correct; when repeated, the frequency of a positive confirmation even rose to more than 50% because the previous figures were similar.

This study demonstrated that the assessment as to whether something is to be judged as correct or fraudulent is essentially dependent on how the situation developed in the past. Something that was fine yesterday is often considered fine today. This is why our Claire from the example assessed the accounts as correct because they looked similar to those in the previous years. However, this similarity may have been faked with fraudulent intent—as was the case in the scandal of the fake balance sheets at Enron; in this case, the responsible auditing firm Arthur Andersen was also convicted for destroying evidence and obstructing justice. When ethics is sliding down a slippery slope, it's sometimes very difficult to notice.

Takeaways

After corporate scandals have been exposed, many people ask themselves how such misconduct stayed undetected for so long. Human perception is mostly based on comparing present to past experience. So if immoral behavior increases gradually over a longer period of time, it's particularly difficult to discover it as it is less likely noticed as such.

References

Gino, F.; Bazerman, M.: (2009) When misconduct goes unnoticed: The acceptability of gradual erosion in others' unethical behavior. Journal of Experimental Social Psychology, 45: 708–719.

CHAPTER 44

People Care More About the Environment When They Know Their Organization Cares Too

The production of goods and services often causes environmental damage. This is why companies are increasingly under social pressure to avoid such negative effects. The example of Virgin Atlantic Airways shows how this can be achieved even in an industry that has been heavily criticized by environmentalists, namely, in aviation. The key is with the pilots.

Caroline works as an aircraft captain for one of the major airlines. She is proud of her work. Week after week she takes hundreds of passengers to their wanted destinations to pursue business or enjoy a vacation. She has been increasingly confronted with criticism from friends and acquaintances in the Green movement, since the aviation industry cannot be seen as climate-neutral in any way, shape, or form. Aviation accounts for around 3% of the annual carbon dioxide emissions. The fact that the aviation industry also handles about 35% of the global trade volume, which creates enormous wealth, plays no role whatsoever for Caroline's friends. For some weeks now, Caroline is at least able to point out to her friends that she is making a small contribution to fuel savings, thereby reducing CO_2 emissions. The airline has initiated a fuel-saving project, but it is Caroline who bears the sole responsibility for its implementation.

The fictitious example of Captain Caroline fits in with a recent study by John A. List of the University of Chicago, conducted with co-authors and in partnership with Virgin Atlantic Airways. The project was about finding a way to make airline captains fly with greater environmental awareness. The general question that goes far beyond the aviation industry is what companies can do to ensure that their employees don't act in an environmentally harmful way. Although penalties and checks are potential tools, the extent of the monitoring can be costly to companies. Are there any simpler means to get employees to avoid a negative impact on the environment?

It may even be financially worthwhile for a company. This is obvious in the aviation industry because fuel savings not only emit less CO_2 but reduce one of the main cost factors for airlines, given that around one-third of the operating costs of airlines are fuel costs.

In 2014, Virgin Atlantic Airways launched a fuel reduction project that is run entirely by the airline pilots. Before take-off, calculations for the optimal fuel load are available, but it is up to the captains whether and, if so, how much fuel they would like to add. More fuel means more weight and thus higher fuel consumption. During the flight, fuel can be saved by economical flying and exploiting winds (similar to consuming more or less gas when driving a car due to different driving styles). After landing, fuel can be saved on the long stretch from the runway to the gate by switching off one of the two engines.

Virgin Atlantic Airways informed all their 335 captains in 2014 that fuel efficiency will be measured on an individual basis over eight months, namely, in all three areas—fueling, during the flight, and after landing up to the gate. One group of captains received monthly analyses of how often the respective goals in saving were achieved. A second group was given monthly target quotas, and a third group had the option of giving money (the airline's) to a charity of their choice when the targets were met. In a reference group, only fuel efficiency was measured, and members of the group were not given any information about it.

A comparison of the figures over the project term in 2014 with those of the same period of the prior year showed that the reference group of captains already had a substantially more efficient fuel consumption in all three areas. This effect is also referred to as the Hawthorne effect, which means that the knowledge of being observed can already change behavior. Although the reference group knew that their data on fuel efficiency was collected, they didn't get any information themselves about it. Nonetheless, fuel efficiency improved. The provision of information (as a first form of intervention) had only a small additional effect. The addition of personal target quotas further improved efficiency, namely, in the same magnitude as the intervention in which the captains could donate some money if they flew more efficiently. In total, the project saved around 1,000 tons of CO_2 and about 500 tons in fuel; these are relatively small amounts, but they were achieved practically without any cost through simple interventions and feedback.

Takeaways

Companies can guide decisions made by their employees in the desired direction by means of suitable incentives. Target agreements and social incentives to behave as wanted can help.

References

Gosnell, G.; List, J.; Metcalfe, R.: (2020) The impact of management practices on employee productivity: A field experiment with airline captains. Journal of Political Economy, 128: 1195–1233.

CHAPTER 45

The Stunted Career Path of Whistleblowers: Employees View Them As Disloyal

*T*he list of corporate scandals is prominent and long. To strengthen the support of ethical conduct at work, many companies adopt a code of ethics and establish "whistle-blowing systems" to uncover criminal or unethical acts. The fact that such systems often do not have the desired effect is largely due to typical human patterns of behavior.*

With hindsight, it's easy to cover up unethical acts. The diesel scandal at VW involved manipulated software used to fake favorable emission values that couldn't be adhered to in reality. After it was uncovered, in media reports, talk shows, and political statements, people expressed their astonishment that the scandal did not become public earlier and that VW employees did not draw attention to the criminal acts early enough so they could have been eliminated at an earlier stage. Such action would have spared VW, its employees, and its customers a great deal of aggravation. Even if exact details—who knew what and when—have not been fully clarified up till now, you have to assume that internally a whole bunch of people must have known about the manipulations going on; nonetheless, it was only the testing conducted by the U.S. Environmental Protection Agency that brought the scandal to light.

What are the reasons why major corporate scandals—at Volkswagen, Enron, Wells Fargo, and many other places—are frequently uncovered only late in the game? Financial aspects are of key import. If huge profits are made through manipulations, companies do everything in their power to prevent discovery. In the case of employees who know about the manipulations and could expose them, loyalty to the company plays a major role.

There is another, very significant dimension as to why employees do not uncover unethical or criminal acts, neither internally (through company channels) nor externally (through the media, e.g.). This dimension has to do with the fact that people who uncover unethical or criminal acts—so-called whistleblowers—practically never have a future in the company concerned. Not only that, a career in another company is also not very likely. Whistleblowers are simply not welcome.

Ernesto Reuben of New York University and Matt Stephenson from Columbia Business School published an article a couple of years ago entitled "Nobody Likes a Rat." Even before Dieselgate at VW, they examined the question of why misconduct in companies goes often unreported and thus is not stopped or stopped much too late. Their study gives insight into why it isn't easy at all to foster ethical conduct and expose misconduct.

In the experimental laboratory study, Reuben and Stephenson began by forming groups of three people, like work groups. Group members could increase their income from the experiment by providing false information, which corresponds to the benefits gained by acts of manipulation. Every member of the group was able to report such wrong statements to a head office, which then imposed financial penalties on the wrongdoers. In one of the test conditions, one of the three members was let go from the work group and had to apply for admission to another group. The application required the unanimous approval of all members of the new group. The vote in that group was based on information given to its members on how often applicants reported misconduct in their previous group and how often they made false statements themselves.

Reuben's experimental study clearly showed that applicants who reported misconduct more frequently were far less likely to be included in the new group. Honesty didn't pay. On the contrary: those who had made false statements more frequently were more likely to be admitted. In other words, the chance of finding a job in another work group was reduced by honest behavior and the reporting of violations.

Whistleblowing—at least in this experiment—is a career killer. When your job and thus your livelihood are jeopardized if you report misconduct, it becomes a lot more comprehensible why many major corporate scandals are exposed quite late, if at all.

The study by Reuben and Stephenson also shows that the members of a different work group more often reject an honest applicant if they themselves had frequently made false statements in the past. It is remarkable that their findings of a laboratory study could be confirmed in real life. Mark Egan of Harvard Business School and his coauthors demonstrated that the market for financial consultants has quite a few black sheep. Although these guys are usually fired after the exposure of illegal activities, they often find a new job, namely, in those companies where the proportion of consultants with documented misconduct is already quite high. Companies that have already displayed misconduct themselves, for example, deliberately giving customers wrong advice or cheating them, attract black sheep.

Since whistleblowers have virtually no future in companies if it's known who they are, many companies have introduced anonymous whistleblowing programs in recent years. In some cases, the anonymous reporting is made to a third party—often a law firm—to reduce the likelihood of the whistleblower being exposed even more. Anonymous systems seem to lead to more reports of illegal acts. But the introduction of anonymous reporting systems also has an unintended side effect. In a number of cases, which is higher than one would like, such plans are used to blacken the reputations of colleagues who might be rivals for the next promotion, for instance. This forces companies to spend considerable amounts of time and money to differentiate between justified reports about wrongdoings and unjustified denunciation.

Takeaways

Whistleblowers are usually celebrated in the media. And they actually do make an indispensable contribution to the uncovering of unethical or criminal acts. But due to typical human behavioral patterns, so-called whistleblower programs often do not work well because people reporting unethical behavior are perceived as traitors.

References

Reuben, E.; Stevenson, M.: (2013) Nobody likes a rat: On the willingness to report lies and the consequences thereof. Journal of Economic Behavior and Organization, 93: 384–391.

Egan, M.; Matvos, G.; Seru, A.: (2019) The market for financial adviser misconduct. Journal of Political Economy 127: 233–295.

CHAPTER 46

A Bad Corporate Culture Can Turn Honest People into Liars

*T*he financial crisis that began in 2007 and is still palpable to-*
day shattered trust in the financial industry and its bankers
permanently. Taking uncontrolled risks, the opaque design
of financial products, and dubious advice given to customers re-
vealed that something had gone awfully wrong in the financial
sector. Does this have anything to do with the corporate culture in
this industry?

In Anne and Even Holt's German thriller *Ventricular Fibril-lation*, Otto Schultz is a top manager in a company that produces implantable defibrillators. He has lost more than $100 million on the stock market because before the onset of the great financial crisis that culminated in the crash of Lehman Brothers, he'd invested everything he had in so-called CDOs (collateralized debt obligations), which became suddenly worthless in the crisis. To get back on his feet, Otto Schultz tries to make up for his losses through criminal activities and speculation. The fact that people with pacemakers are killed is only collateral damage to him (the investigation of the deaths caused by him is the actual content of the thriller). So much for fiction.

In reality, the collateral damage caused by CDOs has also been enormous. In simplified terms, CDOs are securities essentially made up of stocks that are untradeable or are difficult to trade. It's not the underlying securities that are sold but the cash flows arising from them, for example, the repayments of a loan from a simple homeowner in the American Midwest. If suddenly a large number of homeowners are unable to keep up with their installments, for example, because of rising interest, the result is defaults, and the CDOs lose value or become completely worthless. Since the highly risky loan receivables of the CDOs were sold as secure investments, many people lost huge amounts of money and often their livelihoods in the financial crisis.

CDOs and similar securities have therefore been identified as one of the main causes of the financial crisis starting in 2007. What's so scandalous is the fact that leading banks were still selling tons of CDOs to customers, when, internally, the bankers had declared CDOs already as highly risky junk and instructed their underlings to get rid of their own portfolio of CDOs. Bank employees with insider information lied to less well-informed customers about the merits of these investments.

In surveys conducted today on how the public views the honesty of various professions, physicians and priests are ranked high on the list, while bankers invariably bring up the rear. Are bankers dishonest people, or do other factors play a role here, for example, corporate culture? Ernst Fehr from the University of Zurich and his colleagues got to the bottom of this question.

The starting point of their study was the knowledge from sociology and psychology that every person plays different roles in their lives. Someone might be a family man at home, a volunteer in the village's football club, and a customer advisor at a bank. The various roles are defined by different social norms for what behavior is appropriate in a particular role. A father will sometimes give money to his children, while a bank advisor normally will never hand over his own money to customers. This means one and the same person must behave in different ways in different situations depending what role they have at a particular moment.

Fehr and colleagues examined the influence of role identity on honest and dishonest behavior; 128 employees of a major Swiss bank took part in the study, and participants were randomly divided into two groups. The first group initially had to answer several questions about their family situation and leisure activities, while the second group was asked about their professional activities at the bank. The different questions were aimed to activate different roles and thus different norms. Whether they really did was measured as follows: the participants were requested to complete words by entering letters into blank spaces. Here are two examples: "Cap_ _ _ _" and "_ _ ney." The first word might be augmented as "captain" and the second as "honey." Alternatively, "capital" and "money" could be stated. The two groups of participants differed in terms of the frequency with which they chose money-related words. The group with the questions about family and leisure chose them in 25% of cases; those with questions about their work at the bank in about 40% of the cases. The concentration on different roles—family versus bank—thus led to different associations. The influence of the role did not end with the corresponding associations.

In a last step of the study, participants were asked to toss a coin in the air 10 times and catch it and then report how often they got "tails." For each "tails," they got $20 in payment. The study's authors could not see the result of a heads-or-tails toss, so participants were not forced to report their results truthfully. It turned out that the group that was asked about their bank job stated "tails" significantly more often than the group who gave information about their family and leisure activities. Since the probability for "tails" must be identical in both groups, this means that participants who were asked about their role at the bank and whose professional norms were activated lied more frequently.

Fehr concluded that social norms are predominant in the corporate culture of the financial sector that undermine the honesty of employees. Corporate culture thus has an impact on the conduct of people, and this insight does not only apply to the financial, but to all industries.

Takeaways

Corporate culture shapes the behavior in companies because it communicates unwritten rules about what conduct is expected. This is why a corporate culture that signals moral action as a norm is so important for the behavior of its employees toward customers.

References

Cohn, A.; Fehr, E.; Marechal, M.: (2014) Business culture and dishonesty in the banking industry. Nature, 516: 86–89.

PART VIII

Leadership and the C-Suite

CHAPTER 47

Visionary Leaders Outperform Operations-Oriented Leaders Over the Long Term

*T*he CEOs of large companies are in the limelight, earn huge amounts of money, and have enormous power. They work a lot, but what exactly do they spend their time on? Not all of them are doing the same thing, as we shall see. There are essentially two types of CEOs. Which type leads a company plays a role in its success.

During my time at the University of Innsbruck, my colleague Gottfried Tappeiner once told me that one of his sons at the age of 10 asked him what a "boss" actually does all day long. The boy wanted to know because the title of boss intrigued him. Tappeiner, who is very well connected, agreed with a South Tyrolean head of business that his son could spend an entire day with him to learn what being a boss involves. I was pretty impressed with Tappeiner's son showing that type of interest and the father's initiative to furnish an answer. Bosses are often seen as people who exist on some lofty plane, whom you rarely meet, and about whom it's pretty hard to know what they do. After the day with the head of the South Tyrolean company, Tappeiner's son knew that a boss does many different things: talks to employees, negotiates with suppliers and banks, prepares for meetings, walks through the company, attends external business dinners, answers emails (has them answered), and a lot more. The day was an adventure for the kid and gave him detailed knowledge about the day-to-day work of a boss.

Not only are inquisitive children interested in what CEOs do as bosses, the same goes for researchers who want to find out why CEOs are crucial to companies and which of their activities are relevant to corporate success. Oriana Bandiera of the London School of Economics, together with colleagues, looked into the daily routine of more than 1,100 CEOs in six countries (Brazil, Germany, France, the United Kingdom, India, and the United States) and analyzed them in unprecedented detail to identify behavioral patterns and recognize correlations between the conduct of CEOs and the success of their companies.

The CEOs examined came from the manufacturing industry, were 51 years old on average, supervised an average of just over 1,000 employees, and generated an average revenue of more than $200 million a year. For one week, research assistants called the CEOs themselves or their assistants every morning and every evening to record the CEO's schedule. In the morning, it was about the planned daily routine in the evening, about the actual one, each divided into 15-minute units. The following information was collected:

- The type of activity—for example, a meeting, a business lunch, a tour around the company, or time spent in preparation for a meeting
- The duration of an appointment
- The number and positions of participants, for example, whether the appointment was with in-house dialogue partners from certain areas or external people, for example, consultants, suppliers, or customers.

On average, the CEOs spent 70% of their 50-hour work week talking to others (in person, during video conferences, or over the phone). The remaining 30% was applied to preparation and travel. These averages conceal the fact that there were big differences between CEOs, especially when it comes to the frequency of meetings or the number of people at those meetings. Using statistical methods, two types of CEOs were identified from the great amount of data; they were referred to as *managers* and *leaders*, respectively. Managers hold bilateral meetings relatively frequently, are more concerned with production-related aspects, and visit different departments relatively often. Leaders, by contrast, spend more time in meetings involving more than two people, usually executives from different divisions of the company. They are less concerned with operational decisions and more with strategic decisions concerning the company.

The chances of meeting either type of CEO depends, among other things, on the industry in question. Leaders are more at home in major companies, such as multinational corporations, and in industries with higher R&D expenditures. Whether a company is headed by a manager or a leader doesn't depend on the (financial) success of the company prior to the appointment of the current CEO; however, it affects key company metrics after the appointment. Leaders typically head more productive and profitable businesses. On average, better key figures emerge after about three years, which means that the leadership style has a medium-term effect on corporate success.

Bandiera and her colleagues also stress that the findings should not be understood as meaning all enterprises would be more successful if they had a leader as CEO. The type of CEO needs to fit with the company, its culture, and particularly its employees. The fact that frictions often arise when a new CEO is appointed, that there is a lack of congruity, is also explained by the fact that leader CEOs are in shorter supply than manager CEOs, as the data showed. As a result, companies that would do better with a leader often end up with a manager as CEO. The type of CEO at the top of a company has an impact on the company's success.

Takeaways

CEOs have different leadership and management styles. Some can be called strategic leaders; others, managers. Both styles have advantages and disadvantages, but have a measurable impact on corporate success.

References

Bandiera, O.; Prat, A.; Hansen, S.; Sadun, R.: (2020) CEO behavior and firm performance. Journal of Political Economy, 128: 1325–1369.

CHAPTER 48

The Four Traits That Set CEOs Apart from Other Managers: Strategic Thinking, Charisma, Intellectual/Social Skills, and Focus on Results

N *o one would want to claim that CEOs are better people. It is true, however, that they're different from other people. Certain personal traits and skills help on the path from a first-level manager toward the CEO position in a company. What are they?*

Jonathan is excited. He's currently being discussed as the possible CEO of a major, listed company. Initial meetings with the supervisory board went well. Now he must go through an assessment by a management consultancy company. The whole process lasts four hours and is based on a very structured questionnaire. Jonathan's personality traits and his intellectual and social skills ought to be quite evident from the interview. If everything matches the company's requirements profile, the appointment shouldn't be a problem. So that would be the next step in his career, coupled with recognition, influence, and lots of money. Jonathan wonders how he should present himself in the best way during the interview: as a man of action, a strategist, a creative person, an intellectual? After a short period of reflection, he pushes such strategic thoughts to the side. Throughout his career, he did best when he behaved as authentically as possible, the way he actually is. That's how he'll do it again.

The selection of a CEO is an immensely important issue for any company because CEOs determine the course of the company and have a significant influence on its development. Major companies invest a great deal of time and money in searching for a CEO. They frequently also turn to get help from consultants, who specialize in the analysis of personality traits and capability profiles. ghSMART is just such a consultancy firm that regularly carries out assessments of managers for top positions on the board level or directly below. An assessment costs $20,000 or more per candidate. It consists of a half-day interview and a written report on the interview and the candidate of 20 to 40 pages. The questionnaire asks for 30 different qualities that relate to five different areas: leadership skills, personal character traits, intellectual abilities, motivation, and social skills.

Regarding leadership skills, it is asked whether candidates are able to develop employees, for instance, whether they have a wide-ranging professional network, and whether they themselves have hired top people or rather second-class ones. The personal character traits revolve around integrity, organizational skills, decisiveness, and more. Motivation is about endurance, enthusiasm, and the standards of one's own work. As for social skills, the ability to express oneself orally and in writing plays a role, as does dealing with criticism or the ability to solve conflicts and distribute the tasks well on teams. For intellectual abilities, grades and the type of education are important as well as analytical and creative skills.

Steven Kaplan of the University of Chicago and Morten Sorensen of the Copenhagen Business School were given access to 2,600 assessments done by ghSMART and have been able to determine what qualities are most likely helpful for somebody to make it to the board of directors or even to board chairperson. The assessments were made between 2001 and 2013. About one-third of the assessments were carried out for the position of CEO; the remaining ones for other board positions or management positions right below the board level. From the

30 personality traits asked about in the assessment, Kaplan and Sorensen identified four factors in their analysis: general abilities, getting things done, charisma, and strategic thinking.

The group of 2,600 candidates is, in itself, already a very selective, above-average educated, and exceptionally successful group of people. Nonetheless, those who are eligible for or actually become CEOs are clearly different from the others. A person considered for a position as CEO scores well above the others in all four factors: such individuals have better intellectual and social qualities, get things done, have more charisma, and approach tasks more strategically. For the actual appointment as CEO, mainly candidates with better skills, more charisma, and a strategic way of thinking are sought. Getting things done is, at this point, not seen as that significant. By contrast, interpersonal skills are gaining in importance, which express not only "doer qualities," but also prudence, respect, and empathy when dealing with people.

Another rather highly charged detail of the Kaplan and Sorensen study was that women who score as strongly as men in the four factors are still less likely be appointed to be CEOs than men. Discrimination against women at the very top is a factor to be reckoned with. These findings support calls for gender quotas for the C-suites of major corporations.

Takeaways

The journey to the top of a company is a long road. Certain skills and personality traits are essential. CEOs are usually characterized by the ability to get things done, charisma, high cognitive abilities, and a strategic approach to problems.

References

Kaplan, S.; Sorensen, M.: (2021) Are CEOs different? Characteristics of top managers. Journal of Finance, 76, 1773–1811.

CHAPTER 49

Leaders Who Focus on Short-Term Results Innovate Less and Lower Company ROI

*M*aking a company a success needs a long-term perspective. It begins with management. But patience is important not just to executives.

Five hundred entrepreneurs are sitting in the light-filled lecture hall in Telfs in Tyrol, Austria, and listening raptly to the lecturer, Kurt Matzler from Austria's Innsbruck University. His lecture is about the question of whether entrepreneurs in Tyrol are patient and self-disciplined personalities. The audience is spellbound—yet why? You might think there are more exciting topics for entrepreneurs than patience and self-discipline. Kurt Matzler quotes an (unpublished) survey conducted among 259 Tyrolean companies in 2014. Owners, board members, and managing directors were interviewed and asked, among others, how strongly they agree with the following statements:

- "I wish I had more self-discipline."
- "I'm good at resisting temptations."
- "I'm good at working toward long-term goals."

The scale of five possible answers ranged from "Strongly agree" to "Strongly disagree." Along with such questions about personal qualities, data on innovative activity and profitability of their company was collected in the survey. The aim was to find any links between the personal attitudes of top management and the success of their companies.

The survey among Tyrolean companies was motivated by a core message in my own research on the connection between patience and success on an individual level, that is, regardless of the question of what makes companies successful. My core message was brief and concise: patience and self-discipline are enormously important for training, professional success, and the health of an individual; they are of the same importance as the intelligence quotient or family background, for instance.

I became aware of these causal relations initially in a study I did with Martin Kocher, Daniela Glätzle-Rützler, and Stefan Trautmann. Almost 700 young people in Tyrol between the ages of 10 and 18 were asked to choose between a lower sum given immediately and a larger amount doled out in a few weeks. For example, they could pick $10.10 immediately or $11.50 about three weeks later. Such decision-making situations are often used in behavioral economics to measure the level of patience and self-restraint of subjects—forgoing an earlier but not so good option for a better one in the future (I already cited one such study in Chapter 13). Our study in Tyrol showed that those young people who were more willing to wait for a larger amount in the future had better grades, displayed fewer behavioral problems (measured by disciplinary referrals), were less likely to smoke and consume alcohol, and most likely saved some of their allowance.

Other studies—for example from New Zealand, the United States, and Sweden—came to similar conclusions. People with more patience and a higher level of self-discipline are on average better educated (even taking into account the IQ), earn more money, are healthier (being less overweight, smoking and drinking less often, and exercising more), and are significantly less likely to be criminal offenders.

Numerous studies have shown that self-restraint, that is, the ability to resist a short-term temptation for a higher goal in the future, increases the likelihood of success on the level of the individual person. And on the level of companies? This brings me back to the research project by Kurt Matzler mentioned earlier. It turned out that among 259 Tyrolean companies, those whose executives described themselves as more self-disciplined and future-oriented were more innovative on average and had a higher profitability (i.e., returns on investment). Given the large number of studies that examined the link between self-discipline and success on the individual level, such a result stands to reason. Of course, it remains an open question from Kurt Matzler's study whether more profitable and innovative companies hire more patient managers or whether more patient managers turn companies into more profitable and innovative ones, but the relationship suggests that patience and future-oriented thinking of managers is something that helps companies.

Takeaways

> The success of companies depends on all its employees. The personal qualities of board members and managing directors play a role in the innovation and profitability of companies because these qualities have an impact on vital strategic decisions. Companies with more patient board members and managing directors are more successful.

References

Sutter, M.; Kocher, M.; Glätzle-Rützler, D.; Trautmann, S.: (2013) Impatience and uncertainty: Experimental decisions predict adolescents' field behavior. American Economic Review, 103: 510–531.

Moffitt, T. E.; Arseneault, L.; Belsky, D.; et al.: (2011) A gradient of childhood self-control predicts health, wealth, and public safety. Proceedings of the National Acadademy of Sciences of the USA, 108: 2693–2698.

CHAPTER 50

Charismatic Leaders Inspire Their People to Deliver Better Results

*S*teve Jobs is probably the best-known example of a charismatic leader. He was visionary, persuasive, captivating, motivating. Apple's success was widely attributed to the charisma of Jobs. But is charisma really a valuable production factor? Can its impact on productivity be measured at all? Swiss researchers have tried it.

Despite general agreement about the power of Steve Jobs's charisma, it's virtually impossible to use case studies of leaders to assess how a particular company would have developed with a less charismatic leader—because a counterfactual situation is unavailable for comparison. Experimental research, by contrast, can vary the extent of charisma and its impact on the work performance of employees. This is exactly what the Swiss researchers headed by Christian Zehnder from Lausanne University did.

Zehnder and his colleagues were interested in the impact a charismatic speech has on the productivity of employees. The employees were asked to write letters asking for donations to a children's hospital. The task was to pack various items into a large envelope, address the letters, and put them in a big box with the finished envelopes. Before carrying out the task, it was explained to them how the letters were to be done. This explanation was given by a trained actor in two different versions. In the first version, the actor—the employees were unaware that he was an actor—explained all the necessary steps in a neutral tone but emphasized that the call for donations was for a good cause. I'll refer to this version as *neutral speech*. In the second version, the same content was explained by the same speaker but was enriched by techniques that make up charismatic speeches: supportive nonverbal communication, the use of metaphors, anecdotes and rhetorical questions, and the amplification of key items by three arguments each. The ethical context remained the same, but overall the task was presented as important in a far more vivid and convincing way. I'll refer to this version as *charismatic speech*.

In the study, more than 100 employees were hired specifically to complete about 30,000 letters for the donation campaign. A first group (about one-third of the employees) was given the neutral speech to explain the task and a fixed wage of about $25 for three working hours, independent of the number of envelopes they finished. The second group (again about one-third of the employees) was also given the neutral speech, but the participants received about $0.15 per completed envelope in addition to the fixed wage as soon as they exceeded 220 envelopes. The last group listened to the charismatic speech and received, like the first group, a fixed wage of about $25, again independently of the number of envelopes. The comparison of the first group's output (with neutral speech) with that of the third group (with charismatic speech) made it possible to measure the impact on the productivity of a charismatic speech. Then this impact can be compared to the second group that got an additional financial incentive for high work output.

The results left little room for doubt. The charismatic speech led to an increase in work output of around 17% (compared with the output of the first group). This means that the cost per completed letter dropped nearly to the same extent (18%), which was beneficial from the perspective of the pediatric hospital. The second group with the additional financial incentives boosted its output by about 20% compared to the first group. While such an increase was to be expected, the comparison with the third group comes as a surprise at first glance. The increase in output of 17%

by means of charismatic and of 20% by means of additional financial incentives (with the neutral speech) are statistically indistinguishable. This means that a charismatic speech is worth money in the truest sense of the word. In other words, the charismatic explanation of a task has the same motivating impact as additional money for completing the task.

Christian Zehnder and his colleagues were the first to show this effect properly. The study leaves open whether such an effect on productivity of charismatic speeches can be sustained in the long term. The study ended after all 30,000 donation letters had been sent away. Still, it shows that charisma is valuable to companies.

Takeaways

People management is one of the most important tasks of executives. Charismatic leadership motivates employees to achieve higher productivity (even with equal pay).

References

Antonakis, J.; d'Adda, G.; Weber, R.; Zehnder, C.: (2022) Just words? Just speeches? On the economic value of charismatic leadership. Management Science, in press.

Appendix: All Takeaways—For Impatient Readers

To round out the book, you'll find takeaways from each of the 50 chapters here. Each takeaway refers to the situations and studies analyzed in the relevant chapter.

Chapter 1.   It's generally assumed that salary depends on people's skills and previous professional experience. But height also plays a role, at least for men. Taller people build up larger social networks in their late teens and acquire more social skills. This results in higher salaries later in life.

Chapter 2.   Women are evaluated more negatively by men in job interviews if the proportion of women in responsible positions is already relatively high. Therefore, more women on staff selection panels often pose a certain disadvantage for female applicants.

Chapter 3.   Working from home increases productivity in many instances and boosts job satisfaction because it helps sustain the balance between family and work, while eliminating the hassle of the daily commute. However, working from home also entails the risk that promotions will become less likely since networking is a lot more difficult.

Chapter 4.   The more complex the world of work becomes, the more valuable social skills are because jobs increasingly require efficient coordination of team members, facilitating their different wants and ideas and resolving conflicts. Such skills are increasingly rewarded by the labor market and yield better career opportunities and higher salaries.

Chapter 5. Social networks help you get started because valuable information on the opportunities offered on the labor market are conveyed through them. Close contacts are especially helpful, but there are a lot fewer of them than weaker contacts. Training in how to handle social networks can significantly increase career opportunities.

Chapter 6. The usual approach to job placement for an unemployed person starts with providing training for specific professional skills. Alternative approaches using behavioral economics are based on the knowledge that a structured day and reciprocity between the agent and the job seeker are crucial. Job seekers should take this into account when looking for a new job.

Chapter 7. In application processes, the members of selection panels make comparisons between different candidates. The sequence of appearance plays a vital role because it's less likely that earlier candidates get good ratings than later candidates do when no one comes after them. That's why it's more favorable to be interviewed toward the end of the process.

Chapter 8. When looking for a new job, you have to invest a great deal of time and be able to withstand rejection. Impatient people have a harder time coping. This is why they take longer to find a new job than more patient, future-looking people.

Chapter 9. Many newly founded companies disappear from the market after a few years. Survival depends on the composition of the workforce. Startups survive for shorter periods of time if the share of women there is significantly below the average in their industry. A below-average share of women is likely to be a signal for distortions and bias in personnel selection.

Chapter 10.   Filling vacancies is costly. Many companies request that their existing employees give recommendations on who is a good match for a position and a suitable addition to the team. The involvement of existing employees by means of referral programs increases their job satisfaction and the length of time they stay with the company.

Chapter 11.   Human decision-making behavior is subject to errors and distortions. Computer algorithms can help identify the best candidates from among a flood of applications. Taking machine recommendations into consideration may result in an improved selection of personnel and on how long employees stay with the firm.

Chapter 12.   Company loyalty signifies loyalty per se. Frequent job changes are often associated by HR managers with less loyal behavior and less dependability. This is why, if somebody seeks to change jobs, chances of a new position are reduced if they've worked for many different companies in the past.

Chapter 13.   Day-to-day work can be stressful, and new challenges frequently crop up. Certain personal qualities help you not to give in too quickly when confronted with a challenge, but to tackle it and persevere. Patience and long-term thinking are two such valuable qualities.

Chapter 14.   The amount of one's own salary is one of the best kept secrets. For many, this is one of the reasons for gender differences in terms of pay, which is why some employees demand more salary transparency. If salary transparency is introduced for top positions in administration, it actually leads to more salary compression but makes it more difficult to fill senior positions.

Chapter 15. The relationship between managers and employees influences the working atmosphere as well as productivity. Discriminatory behavior by managers results in a reduced work performance even if discrimination manifests only in the fact that the manager has less contact with certain employees.

Chapter 16. When weighing the pros and cons of a given decision, external factors such as heat, humidity, and such play no role from a traditional point of view. Such factors have a measurable impact on human decisions, though, since they affect the mood and risk appetite of people.

Chapter 17. Executives today are expected to communicate in a transparent manner what is expected when it comes to their employees' work performance, to give regular feedback, to promote their employees' careers, and to provide guidance and advice. People who have these skills are better able to "manage" people, thus reducing employee churn and heightening job satisfaction.

Chapter 18. In many industries, customers know less about the products sold and their quality than the company selling them. This is why the trustworthiness of employees plays a crucial role in the public perception of an industry, and hiring procedures should take this into account.

Chapter 19. Social norms influence human decision-making in every situation of life. Something perceived as appropriate behavior rubs off on other people's own behavior. This is true in professional life as well. It's of relevance in this context whether one's own behavior can be observed. If this is the case, your work performance adapts to those peers who can observe you.

Chapter 20. More and more companies are committing to a defined mission and creating a catalog of values to which they pledge themselves. But if the people working there cannot identify with the mission, work performance is impeded owing to a lack of motivation.

Chapter 21. Work teams depend on each member making an effort toward the team's success. People cooperate more frequently, the more they expect and perceive cooperation from others. This conditional cooperation means that teams with many cooperative members are more successful and productive overall.

Chapter 22. On work teams, various tasks must be assigned as efficiently as possible to single members to be successful as a team. When all team members have a say on the distribution of the tasks, motivation is heightened and cooperation is improved.

Chapter 23. People imitate the behavior of others who are important in their lives. This tendency for imitation makes leadership in a company crucial. If executives don't just talk the talk but walk the walk, employees will do the same.

Chapter 24. Many people cooperate on a team if the other members cooperate as well. This human trait of conditional cooperation makes setting a good example such an important tool to improve the productivity of work teams.

Chapter 25. Behavioral economists have found that women are usually more reluctant to compete with others, compared to men. This has implications for the careers of the two sexes. Quotas could motivate the best-qualified women to compete, thus improving their chances for advancement. The concern about underqualified "quota women" does not square with the empirical evidence.

Chapter 26. Willingness to compete with others has an important influence on training and career decisions early in life. More competitive people tend to choose professions where they can earn more money later and are more likely to apply for jobs where competition plays a role.

Chapter 27. Gender differences in competitive behavior help to explain gender differences existing on the labor markets. But it's not only in adulthood that men and women differ in terms of willingness to compete. The differences are already pronounced in early childhood, are related to children's families, and have very long-term effects.

Chapter 28. Our behavior is shaped by the culture in which we grow up and do things. Expectations placed upon the behavior of men and women are also culturally conditioned, and this matters for labor market outcomes.

Chapter 29. Explanations for the fact that men, on average, earn more money than women are numerous and multifold. Some of the gender differences can be attributed to men being more assertive in salary negotiations than women and asking more frequently for a higher salary. But when it's clear that the salary can be negotiated, these gender differences in salary negotiations vanish.

Chapter 30. Although the number of women at the top of companies has been rising slowly, their increasing presence in the C suite has produced impressive results. Women as directors or CEOs influence the salary distribution and productivity in companies.

Chapter 31. In a company, not every work step or every decision of employees can be monitored. This is why trust is so important for efficient collaboration. The level of trust in a society correlates with its economic prosperity.

Chapter 32. A degree of supervision is not harmful to employment relationships. Monitoring mechanisms destroy trust only if they are applied permanently.

If monitoring possibilities exist but employers apply them less and give their employees an advance in trust, the mutual trust relationship is strengthened.

Chapter 33. People don't care only about themselves. This means that the question of how other people are treated in a company is important for the behavior and work performance of individuals. Unfair behavior by employers has a negative impact on the motivation and productivity of employees, even if they're not directly impacted by the unfair behavior.

Chapter 34. Nudging with appeals to fairness can help establish sound relationships between companies and customers. If communicated properly, the appeals create a positive "Tit for tat" spirit that improves payment morale.

Chapter 35. In the past, the idea was widespread that better pay results in better decisions by employees. However, better pay can be a burden and even impede cognitive processes. So decisions don't automatically get any better if more money is paid for good decisions.

Chapter 36. If the contribution of individual team members to the output of the entire team is hard to measure, companies can introduce a team bonus. It improves the performance of the entire team because work processes are coordinated better and productivity is increased.

Chapter 37. Bonus payments are designed to motivate people to perform better. However, it can backfire if the bonus payments violate reference points for what is considered a just allotment of bonuses. They can then have a negative impact on job satisfaction and productivity.

Chapter 38. Most major companies have relative pay schemes in which a higher output is rewarded with more money. As soon as notions of fairness are violated by such systems, output may go down instead of being increased.

Chapter 39. When companies use relative pay schemes, they give their employees a strong incentive to take greater risks in their work to outperform others. In extreme cases, this can ruin the whole company.

Chapter 40. Companies depend on people working well together. If individual employees can earn more money if they are considered more productive than others, such relative payment systems create incentives for somebody sabotaging the efforts of others.

Chapter 41. Markets are characterized by high gains in efficiency. Market-based action also makes people less ethical than when acting alone. This must be taken into account for both individual companies and society as a whole.

Chapter 42. Many situations in day-to-day work have a moral dimension. How people balance ethics and financial advantages depends on the consequences their actions have for themselves and for others. The frequency of immoral behavior depends on the costs and benefits of an action.

Chapter 43. After corporate scandals have been exposed, many people ask themselves how such misconduct stayed undetected for so long. Human perception is mostly based on comparing present to past experience. So if immoral behavior increases gradually over a longer period of time, it's particularly difficult to discover it as it is less likely noticed as such.

Chapter 44. Companies can guide decisions made by their employees in the desired direction by means of suitable incentives. Target agreements and social incentives to behave as wanted can help.

Chapter 45. Whistleblowers are usually celebrated in the media. And they actually do make an indispensable contribution to the uncovering of unethical or criminal acts. But due to typical human behavioral patterns, so-called whistleblower programs often do not work well because people reporting unethical behavior are perceived as traitors.

Chapter 46. Corporate culture shapes the behavior in companies because it communicates unwritten rules about what conduct is expected. This is why a corporate culture that signals moral action as a norm is so important for the behavior of its employees toward customers.

Chapter 47. CEOs have different leadership and management styles. Some can be called strategic leaders; others, managers. Both styles have advantages and disadvantages, but have a measurable impact on corporate success.

Chapter 48. The journey to the top of a company is a long road. Certain skills and personality traits are essential. CEOs are usually characterized by the ability to get things done, charisma, high cognitive abilities, and a strategic approach to problems.

Chapter 49. The success of companies depends on all its employees. The personal qualities of board members and managing directors play a role in the innovation and profitability of companies because these qualities have an impact on vital strategic decisions. Companies with more patient board members and managing directors are more successful.

Chapter 50. People management is one of the most important tasks of executives. Charismatic leadership motivates employees to achieve higher productivity (even with equal pay).

Source Materials

The following are the original academic publications for each chapter, to which I refer explicitly in the corresponding chapters.

Chapter 1. Persico, N.; Postlewaite, A.; Silverman, D.: (2004) The effect of adolescent experience on labor market outcomes: The case of height. Journal of Political Economy, 112: 1019–1051.

Chapter 2. Bagues, M.; Sylos-Labini, M.; Zinovyeva, N.: (2017) Does the gender composition of scientific committees matter? American Economic Review, 107: 1207–1238.
Goldin, C.; Rouse, C.: (2000) Orchestrating impartiality: The impact of "blind" auditions on female musicians. American Economic Review, 90: 715–741.

Chapter 3. Bloom, N.; Liang, J.; Roberts, J.; Ying, Z. J.: (2015) Does working from home work? Evidence from a Chinese experiment. Quarterly Journal of Economics, 130: 165–218.
Emanuel, N.; Harrington, E.: (2021) "Working" remotely? Selection, treatment and the market provision of remote work. Working Paper. Harvard University.

Chapter 4. Deming, D.: (2017) The growing importance of social skills in the labor market. Quarterly Journal of Economics, 132: 1593–1640.

Chapter 5. Gee, L. K.; Jones, J.; Burke, M.: (2017) Social networks and labor markets: How strong ties relate to job finding on Facebook's social network. Journal of Labor Economics, 35: 485–518.
Wheeler, L.; Garlick, R.; Johnson, E.; Shaw, P.; Gargano, M.: (2022) LinkedIn (to) job opportunities: Experimental evidence from job readiness training. American Economic Journal: Applied Economics, 14: 101–125.

Chapter 6. Abel, M.; Burger, R.; Carranza, E.; Piraino, P.: (2019) Bridging the intention-behavior gap? The effect of plan-making prompts on job search and employment. American Economic Journal: Applied Economics, 11: 284–301.

Chapter 7. Ginsburgh, V.; van Ours, J.: (2003) Expert opinion and compensation: Evidence from a musical competition. American Economic Review, 93: 289–296.

Chapter 8. DellaVigna, S.; Paserman, M.: (2005) Job search and impatience. Journal of Labor Economics, 23: 527–588.

Chapter 9. Weber, A.; Zulehner, C.: (2010) Female hires and success of start-ups. American Economic Review, Papers and Proceedings, 100: 358–361.

Chapter 10. Friebel, G.; Heinz, M.; Hoffman, M.; Zubanov, N.: (2022) What do employee referral programs do? Journal of Political Economy, in press.

Chapter 11. Hoffman, M.; Kahn, L.; Li, D.: (2018) Discretion in hiring. Quarterly Journal of Economics, 133: 765–800.

Chapter 12. Cohn, A.; Marechal, M.; Schneider, F.; Weber, R. A.: (2021) Frequent job changes can signal poor work attitude and reduce employability. Journal of the European Economic Association, 19: 475–508.

Chapter 13. Burks, S.; Carpenter, J.; Goette, L.; Rustichini, A.: (2009) Cognitive skills affect economic preferences, strategic behavior, and job attachment. Proceedings of the National Academy of Sciences, 106: 7745–7750.

Chapter 14. Mas, A.: (2017) Does transparency lead to pay compression? Journal of Political Economy, 125: 1683–1721

Chapter 15. Glover, D.; Pallais, A.; Pariente, W.: (2017) Discrimination as self-fulfilling prophecy: Evidence from French Grocery Stores. Quarterly Journal of Economics, 132: 1219–1260.

Chapter 16. Heyes, A.; Saberian, S.: (2019) Temperature and decisions: Evidence from 207,000 court cases. American Economic Journal: Applied Economics, 11: 238–265.

Chapter 17. Hoffman, M.; Tadelis, S.: (2021) People management skills, employee attrition, and manager rewards: An empirical analysis. Journal of Political Economy, 129: 243–285.

Chapter 18. Gill, A.; Heinz, M.; Schumacher, H.; Sutter, M.: (2022) Trustworthiness in the financial industry. Management Science, in press.

Chapter 19. Mas, A.; Moretti, E.: (2009) Peers at work. American Economic Review, 99: 112–145.

Chapter 20. Carpenter, J.; Gong, E.: (2016) Motivating agents: How much does the mission matter? Journal of Labor Economics, 34: 211–236.

Chapter 21. Carpenter, J.; Seki, E.: (2011) Do social preferences increase productivity? Field experimental evidence from fishermen in Toyama Bay. Economic Inquiry, 49: 612–630.

Chapter 22. Chan, D.: (2016) Teamwork and moral hazard: Evidence from the emergency department. Journal of Political Economy, 124: 734–770.

Sutter, M.; Haigner, S.; Kocher, M.: (2010) Choosing the stick or the carrot?—Endogenous institutional choice in social dilemma situations. Review of Economic Studies, 77: 1540–1566.

Chapter 23. Johnson, R.: (2015) Leading by example: Supervisor modeling and officer-initiated activities. Police Quarterly, 18: 223–243.

Chapter 24. Güth, W.; Levati, M. V.; Sutter, M.; van der Heijden, E.: (2007) Leading by example with and without exclusion power in voluntary contribution experiments. Journal of Public Economics, 91: 1023–1042.

Sutter, M.; Rivas, F.: (2014), Leadership, reward, and punishment in sequential public goods experiments. In: van Lange, P.; Rockenbach, B.; Yamagishi, T. (Eds): Reward and Punishment in Social Dilemmas. Oxford University Press, Oxford, 133–160.

Chapter 25. Balafoutas, L.; Sutter, M.: (2012) Affirmative action policies promote women and do not harm efficiency in the lab. Science, 335: 579–582.

Niederle, M.; Segal C.; Vesterlund, L.: (2013) How costly is diversity? Affirmative action in light of gender differences in competitiveness. Management Science, 59: 1–16.

Chapter 26. Buser, T.; Niederle, M.; Oosterbeek, H.: (2014) Gender, competitiveness, and career choices. Quarterly Journal of Economics, 129: 1409–1447.

Flory, J.; Leibbrandt, A.; List, J.: (2015) Do competitive workplaces deter female workers? A large-scale natural field experiment on job entry decisions. Review of Economic Studies, 82: 122–155.

Niederle, M.; Vesterlund, L.: (2007) Do women shy away from competition? Do men compete too much? Quarterly Journal of Economics, 122: 1067–1101

Chapter 27. Sutter, M.; Glätzle-Rützler, D.: (2015) Gender differences in the willingness to compete emerge early in life and persist. Management Science, 61: 2339–2354.

Almas, I.; Cappelen, A.; Salvanes, K. G. et al.: (2016) Willingness to compete: Family matters. Management Science, 62: 2149–2162.

Chapter 28. Gneezy, U.; Leonard, K.; List, J.: (2009) Gender differences in competition: Evidence from a matrilineal and a patriarchal society. Econometrica, 77: 1637–1664.

Chapter 29. Leibbrandt, A.; List, J.: (2015) Do women avoid salary negotiations? Evidence from a large-scale natural field experiment. Management Science, 61: 2016–2024.

Babcock, L.; Laschever, S.: (2003) Women Don't Ask: Negotiation and the Gender Divide. Princeton University Press.

Chapter 30. Flabbi, L.; Macis, M.; Moro, A.; Schivardi, F.: (2019) Do female executives make a difference? The impact of female leadership on gender gaps and firm performance. Economic Journal, 129: 2390–2423.

Chapter 31. Sutter, M.; Kocher, M.: (2007) Trust and trustworthiness across different age groups. Games and Economic Behavior 59: 364–382.

Knack, S.; Keefer, P.: (1997) Does social capital have an economic payoff? A cross-country investigation. Quarterly Journal of Economics, 112: 1251–1288.

Chapter 32. Fehr, E.; List, J.: (2004) The hidden costs and returns of incentives—Trust and trustworthiness among CEOs. Journal of the European Economic Association, 2: 743–771.

Chapter 33. Heinz, M.; Jeworrek, S.; Mertins, V. et al.: (2020) Measuring indirect effects of unfair employer behavior on worker productivity—A field experiment. Economic Journal, 130: 2546–2568.

Dube, A.; Giuliano, L.; Leonard, J.: (2019) Fairness and frictions: The impact of unequal raises on quit behavior. American Economic Review, 109: 620–663.

Chapter 34. Sutter, C.; Rosenberger, W.; Sutter, M.: (2020) Nudging with your child's education. A field experiment on collecting municipal dues when enforcement is scant. Economics Letters, 191: 109–116.

Chapter 35. Ariely, D.; Gneezy, U.; Loewenstein, G.; Mazar, N.: (2009) Large stakes and big mistakes. Review of Economic Studies, 76: 451–469.

Dohmen, T.: (2008) Do professionals choke under pressure. Journal of Economic Behavior and Organization, 65: 636–653.

Chapter 36. Friebel, G.; Heinz, M.; Krüger, M.; Zubanov, N.: (2017) Team incentives and performance: Evidence from a retail chain. American Economic Review, 107: 2168–2203.

Chapter 37. Ockenfels, A.; Sliwka, D.; Werner, P.: (2015) Bonus payments and reference point violations. Management Science, 61: 1496–1513.

Chapter 38. Bandiera, O.; Barankay, I.; Rasul, I.: (2005) Social preferences and the response to incentives: Evidence from personnel data. Quarterly Journal of Economics, 100: 917–961.

Chapter 39. Kirchler, M.; Lindner, F.; Weitzel, U.: (2018) Rankings and risk-taking in the finance industry. Journal of Finance, 73: 2271–2302.

Chapter 40. Harbring, C.; Irlenbusch, B.: (2011) Sabotage in tournaments: Evidence from a laboratory experiment. Management Science, 57: 611–627.

Chapter 41. Falk, A.; Szech, N.: (2013) Morals and markets. Science, 340: 707–711.
Kirchler, M.; Huber, J.; Stefan, M.; Sutter, M.: (2016) Market design and moral behavior. Management Science, 62: 2615–2625.

Chapter 42. Gneezy, U.: (2005) Deception: The role of consequences. American Economic Review, 95: 384–394.

Chapter 43. Gino, F.; Bazerman, M.: (2009) When misconduct goes unnoticed: The acceptability of gradual erosion in others' unethical behavior. Journal of Experimental Social Psychology, 45: 708–719.

Chapter 44. Gosnell, G.; List, J.; Metcalfe, R.: (2020) The impact of management practices on employee productivity: A field experiment with airline captains. Journal of Political Economy, 128: 1195–1233.

Chapter 45. Reuben, E.; Stevenson, M.: (2013) Nobody likes a rat: On the willingness to report lies and the consequences thereof. Journal of Economic Behavior and Organization, 93: 384–391.
Egan, M.; Matvos, G.; Seru, A.: (2019) The market for financial adviser misconduct. Journal of Political Economy, 127: 233–295.

Chapter 46. Cohn, A.; Fehr, E.; Marechal, M.: (2014) Business culture and dishonesty in the banking industry. Nature, 516: 86–89.

Chapter 47. Bandiera, O.; Prat, A.; Hansen, S.; Sadun, R.: (2020) CEO behavior and firm performance. Journal of Political Economy, 128: 1325–1369.

Chapter 48. Kaplan, S.; Sorensen, M.: (2021) Are CEOs different? Characteristics of top managers. Journal of Finance, 76, 1773–1811.

Chapter 49. Sutter, M.; Kocher, M.; Glätzle-Rützler, D.; Trautmann, S.: (2013) Impatience and uncertainty: Experimental decisions predict adolescents' field behavior. American Economic Review, 103: 510–531.

Moffitt, T. E.; Arseneault, L.; Belsky, D., et al.: (2011) A Gradient of Childhood Self-Control Predicts Health, Wealth, and Public Safety. Proceedings of the National Acadademy of Sciences of the USA, 108: 2693–2698.

Chapter 50. Antonakis, J.; d'Adda, G.; Weber, R.; Zehnder, C.: (2022) Just words? Just speeches? On the economic value of charismatic leadership. Management Science, in press.

About the Author

Matthias Sutter is the director of the Max Planck Institute for Research on Collective Goods in Bonn. There, he heads the Experimental Economics Group. As a professor for experimental economic research, he teaches at the Universities of Cologne and Innsbruck. After graduating with a major in theology, he studied economics at Innsbruck University, where he graduated and qualified as a professor. Subsequently, he was the research group director at the Max Planck Institute for Economics in Jena, and later had professorships in Gothenburg and Florence (at the European University Institute).

Matthias Sutter was born in Austria. With more than 130 peer-reviewed publications (among others, in *Science*, *Nature Communications*, the *American Economic Review*, the *Quarterly Journal of Economics*, or the *Journal of Political Economy*), he is one of the most productive economists in the German-speaking region. He does research on the development of economic preferences in children and young people, the advantages of team decisions, and behavioral economic aspects of professional life.

He became known to the wider German public with his bestseller *Die Entdeckung der Geduld* (2nd edition, 2018, with Ecowin) that led to his being the guest on many talk shows, on radio programs, and in the cultural and entertainment section of newspapers. Matthias Sutter is a much sought after speaker in companies and public organizations. His experience as an actor during his time at university is of great advantage to him. On the studio stage of Innsbruck University, he played the leading role in Goethe's *Torquato Tasso* at the Tyrolean State Theatre. But because he thought an acting career was far too risky (and didn't think himself sufficiently talented), he opted for an academic career, which he has been pursuing with passion to this day.

Index